Chile: Prospects for Democracy

✧

Chile: Prospects for Democracy

Mark Falcoff
Arturo Valenzuela
Susan Kaufman Purcell

Council on Foreign Relations
New York

COUNCIL ON FOREIGN RELATIONS BOOKS

The Council on Foreign Relations, Inc., is a nonprofit and non-partisan organization devoted to promoting improved understanding of international affairs through the free exchange of ideas. The Council does not take any position on questions of foreign policy and has no affiliation with, and receives no funding from, the United States government.

From time to time, books and monographs written by members of the Council's research staff or visiting fellows, or commissioned by the Council, or written by an independent author with critical review contributed by a Council study or working group are published with the designation "Council on Foreign Relations Book." Any book or monograph bearing that designation is, in the judgment of the Committee on Studies of the Council's board of directors, a responsible treatment of a significant international topic worthy of presentation to the public. All statements of fact and expressions of opinion contained in Council books are, however, the sole responsibility of the author.

ISBN: 0-87609-045-5

Contents

Foreword

The renewal of democratic government that has swept across so much of Latin America in the 1980s is a phenomenon of historic proportion.

Rightly, the United States has taken a good deal of satisfaction from this revitalization of the democratic spirit in the Western Hemisphere. It is undeniably in our national interest to have more democracies in Latin America. Such countries share with us a commitment to the principles of accountability and transparency as organizing concepts of government. They tend to have views similar to our own on such questions as how international disputes should be settled, how their economies should be organized, and how international trade and commerce should be conducted.

For all of the disorder and occasional lack of coherence that characterize democracies—including our own—countries with democratic governments make far better neighbors than those with non-democratic governments. They are far less likely to engage in external adventurism, and they are on the whole far more successful in meeting the social and economic aspirations of their own citizens.

Moreover, our support for democracy has proven to be a unifying force in our own foreign policy. To the extent that the goals and means of our foreign policy can be shown to be rooted in the democratic principles and values on which our own system of government is based, we are more able to maintain the sort of bipartisan political support on which the successful conduct of U.S. foreign policy depends.

Yet, the United States would do well to exercise considerable restraint in claiming credit for the progress of recent years in the restoration of Latin American democracy. Because of the demonology that surrounds so much of what we say and do in Latin America, any tendency on our part to claim a pivotal role in the restoration of democracy tends, perversely, to weaken those moderate forces in still-fragile democracies which are trying to build institutions on the narrow middle ground between the extremes of right and left.

Moreover, while the United States did, in most cases, say and do the right things in Latin America over the past several years, our actual role in the restoration of democratic institutions was a secondary one. The massive marshalling of popular will that brought democracy back to these countries was a force whose leadership and energy came from within. It was not somehow stimulated and directed from the outside.

On the other hand, to the extent that U.S. support for democracy strengthens and encourages political moderates striving to rebuild democratic institutions, we obviously play a significant role. Moreover, if after democratic renewal has been successful, the people and political leadership of a given country perceive that the United States has been supportive, our long-term relationship and interests clearly benefit.

The renewal of democratic government is not, however, a universal phenomenon in Latin America. Chile, along with Nicaragua, Cuba, and a few others, stands out as a country in which the principles of accountability and transparency clearly are not being applied.

Chile also stands out as an example of the difficult choices of substance and timing that repeatedly confront the United States as it tries to use its influence in helping to bring about a return to democratic institutions.

The three excellent essays in this book provide illuminating insights into the extraordinarily complicated political situation in Chile, the rigidities produced by decades of ideological strife, and the tremendous difficulties in forming a working consensus in support of peaceful democratic change within the Chilean body politic. They also describe starkly the paucity of options available to the United States in a situation in which, rightly or wrongly, perceptions of American power and responsibility may be far greater than our actual ability to bring our influence to bear in a constructive manner.

Stephen W. Bosworth

Preface

After 15 years of military rule, Chileans are preparing to vote in a national plebiscite for or against the establishment of a form of limited democracy under the continued tutelage of the military. If the majority votes no, under the terms of the 1980 constitution, competitive elections will be held within a year. During that time, however, General Augusto Pinochet Ugarte will continue to occupy the presidency.

Although most Chileans are moderate and democratic, public opinion polls show them to be divided over the desirability of returning the military to the barracks and restoring full democracy. In part, this reflects their uncertainty as to whether a return to democracy would also imply a return to the political instability and economic deterioration that characterized the Allende years. The fact that the democratic opposition to the Pinochet regime has been unable to coalesce around a single leader adds to their uneasiness. Finally, considerable numbers of people who in theory support democracy have benefited substantially by the past five years of economic growth and are therefore inclined to vote for "the devil they know."

At the same time, however, it seems doubtful that those Chileans who favor a restoration of full democracy will accept the defeat of that option in a plebiscite managed by a regime that they regard as illegitimate. Their opposition to a continuation of Pinochet's rule, whether direct or indirect, makes it unlikely that the political and economic stability of the past several years will continue into the future.

Chile is therefore at an important crossroads. The way the country confronts the challenges that lie immediately ahead will determine in great part the path it will take for the remainder of the century.

The United States is on record as supporting the restoration of democracy in Chile. Yet, despite the perceptions of most

Chileans, the ability of the United States to bring about its desired goal is limited. The United States is not without influence. The problem is that decisions taken by the U.S. president or Congress could have unintended consequences in Chile that could substantially harm the interests of both Chileans and the United States.

The three essays in this volume have each been written by experienced analysts of Chilean politics and the policy-making process in the United States. The lead essay by Mark Falcoff, entitled "Chile: A Cognitive Map," argues that Chilean society remains divided into the same three groups that led to the breakdown of the democratic political system in 1973. Falcoff goes on to describe the composition and views of these groups, as well as the nature and disposition of the military, a "fourth" group, and concludes that the political stakes in Chile will be very high during the next few months, with no group likely to achieve a clear victory.

In the second essay, "The 1988–89 Plebiscite in Chile: Political Scenarios for the Future," Arturo Valenzuela predicts that the no vote in the plebiscite will be larger than the yes vote (assuming the plebiscite is held), since Chile's democratic tradition is producing growing resistance to continued military rule. Even if the government is defeated, however, Valenzuela believes that the road to democracy will be rocky unless the democratic opposition unites around a single candidate.

The last essay, by Susan Kaufman Purcell, compares the different approaches used by the Carter and Reagan administrations toward the Pinochet regime in their efforts to help Chile return to democratic rule and argues that neither approach succeeded in changing Pinochet's behavior. She concludes by noting that if Pinochet continues to rule Chile beyond the expiration of his current term, pressure within the United States in favor of harsher sanctions will increase, despite the fact that such sanctions may do more harm than good.

Acknowledgements

This book is the product of the combined efforts of a number of individuals and organizations. The authors wish to thank Ambassador Stephen W. Bosworth for the excellent job he did in chairing the meetings of the Chile Study Group, where the papers in this volume were first presented. We are also grateful to the members of the study group for their insightful comments. Stephanie Golob, Assistant to the Director of the Latin American Project at the Council, made an invaluable contribution by helping to organize and run the meetings of the study group, providing important substantive and editorial suggestions on the manuscript and serving as rapporteur at the study group meetings, as did Theodore Piccone, whom we also wish to thank. Patricia Ravalgi, formerly Assistant to the Director of the Latin American Project, played an important role in helping to launch the study group, while Sue Roach did an admirable job in transcribing and helping to edit the various versions of the papers. We greatly benefited from the thoughtful, constructive and detailed suggestions of Ambassador William Luers and Professor Paul Sigmund, who read the manuscript. Dore Hollander's excellent editing of the final versions of the essays is also greatly appreciated. William Gleysteen, the Council's Vice President for Studies, and David Kellogg and Jeremy Brenner of the Council's publication office, also offered useful advice.

This publication, and the Chile Study Group on which it is based, were made possible by generous grants to the Latin American Project of the Council on Foreign Relations by the Ford Foundation, the Andrew W. Mellon Foundation, the Smith Richardson Foundation and the Tinker Foundation.

Mark Falcoff
Arturo Valenzuela
Susan Kaufman Purcell

August 1988

Latin America

Chile: Prospects for Democracy

CHILE: A COGNITIVE MAP

Mark Falcoff

Chile's return to democracy is by no means assured. The society remains divided into the same three groups that led to the breakdown of the democratic political system in 1973. The right would like to turn the clock back to the mid-1930s or before, but since this is impossible, prefers continued military rule. The left is divided. There are those who would like a situation in which many of the themes of the Allende experiment could be resumed—this time with a genuine commitment to democracy and the rule of law. The revolutionary left would like the creation of a full-blown revolutionary state of the kind found in Cuba or Nicaragua. The center, dominated by the Christian Democrats, would like the establishment of a centrist reform government reminiscent of the Frei administration. The armed forces continue to back Pinochet because they wish to retain their privileges, fear being tried for human rights abuses, distrust what democracy has historically produced in Chile and are apprehensive about the uncertainty that a restored democratic system would bring.

An American diplomat who recently returned from Chile described the country as a "Platonic republic." What he had in mind, evidently, was the climate of order and normality, even modest prosperity, which is so different from the country's international image and from the situation in some neighboring republics. Yet beneath the surface calm there is a pervasive uncertainty about the nation's future, a sensation that becomes more explicit as it approaches 1989. How Chile manages the political challenges that lie immediately in front of it will determine much of its immediate future and, inevitably, the quality of its relations with the United States.

3

Stated somewhat telegraphically, Chile today is ruled by a military dictatorship, though almost yesterday it was the oldest and firmest democratic society in Latin America. Also, it possesses the largest, best-organized, and most committed Communist party in the entire hemisphere. A combination of this sort suggests that under certain circumstances Chile could conceivably move without serious interruption from one form of dictatorship to another. On the other hand, repeated polls show that public opinion is overwhelmingly moderate and democratic. The parties of the broad center probably account for 60-70 percent of the electorate. Unfortunately, no single party or leader can claim to speak for more than a third of this public; even if that were not so, it is difficult to imagine how—under present arrangements—this trend could find effective political expression.

As things stand now, Chile is due sometime before March 1989—but probably in October or November 1988—to go to plebiscite over the continuance, indeed the perpetuation, of its present system. If the current military dictator, Augusto Pinochet Ugarte, manages to negotiate his way over this, his final political hurdle, he will have won an important tactical victory—but unless his margin is very large, Chile's problems of political fragmentation and the questions surrounding the legitimacy of the government will remain unresolved. In that event, the major political variable will remain the degree to which Pinochet can draw his opponents into meaningful participation in his system (and the degree to which the opposition is willing to settle for something less than genuine democracy). Nothing in Pinochet's personal history, or in the history of relations between him and his opponents, suggests that either of these eventualities is likely. Under such circumstances, the far left could conceivably become the chief beneficiary of a prolonged political stalemate. In addition, Pinochet's "reelection" after fifteen years in power would naturally accentuate the already deep personalist strains within the regime; thus, in the best of cases, Chile might be left adrift once he is gone.

Recent polls suggest that if the plebiscite is conducted honestly, Pinochet (or some other candidate designated by the junta) will lose. But even if that is allowed to occur, the rules call for him to remain as president for another year, and as commander in chief of the army, indefinitely. Competitive elections would be held in 1990, after which the successful contender would be required to govern according to rules established by the defeated military party,[1] which presumably would be in a position to enforce them. Opposition leaders frequently pass over this problem by saying that after the plebiscite they will "negotiate with the armed forces"— that is, they will reach an agreement to change the system entirely. Whether this happens, however, depends upon the number voting no, the disposition of the armed forces, the degree to which they interpret Pinochet's defeat as a signal that the nation's course must be changed, and the conduct of the opposition during the interim period. Thus, in either case, Chile's political future is difficult to predict.

Nor can a "wild card" scenario be excluded, in which Pinochet and the armed forces, foreseeing a humiliating defeat in the plebiscite, choose to cancel or postpone it.[2] This would be a very serious break with the regime's own institutionality, and would undoubtedly shatter what remains of its political credibility. Although the domestic political costs could prove to be incalculably high, Pinochet has displayed a remarkable ability to ride out momentary storms; if his prospects of winning the plebiscite continue to narrow, this approach may well gain official favor.

A Dilemma for the Right

One way of understanding the present situation in Chile is to show how it appears to the broad ideological and political families there—the right, the center, the left, and what has become a virtual fourth partner in the game, the armed forces. Each has a different collective memory of the past, and each possesses a different idealized vision of the future. The issue is not whether any one group's notions need be accepted *in toto* but, rather, to what degree one can conceptualize a reasonably civilized synthesis.

Any serious analysis of the right in Chile requires the same kind of careful distinctions that most people automatically accord to the left. As an organized political force, it probably accounts for no more than 20 percent of the electorate in the best of times; in the twilight of the Pinochet regime, it is bound to represent somewhat less. Yet the right still deserves to be taken fully into account, if for no other reason than that it represents some of the most able, serious, disciplined, and sophisticated members of Chilean society. These are the people with advanced degrees from foreign universities; who speak English, French, and German well; who have traveled and lived outside of Chile and therefore have a cosmopolitan worldview; who have extensive business, personal, and political contacts in the major Western countries. Historically, the right in Chile has controlled the press and the electronic media and, in contrast to its counterparts in other Latin American countries, has been well represented in the universities and other cultural institutions.

But the right in Chile is more than this. In the smaller villages and towns, particularly in the north and south, it represents to many men and women the political expression of a deep longing for security of property and for bourgeois respectability. Others comfortably situated in post-industrial societies may scorn or reject such feelings, but these sentiments constitute a serious and often overlooked factor in Chile's political equation.

The right is also the chief beneficiary of disillusionment with reformist governments, or fear of the left. Twice in recent Chilean history it has recovered from near oblivion by way of simple reaction—once against the Christian Democrats (1968–69), once against Allende's Popular Unity (1972–73). In a small society of limited material possibilities, it is always difficult to give to some without taking from others. While all reform parties in Chile (as elsewhere) have spoken of this as if it were a simple matter, none have found it so in practice. This situation explains the country's history of heavy foreign borrowing, and underlines the truth of one observation made by a Christian Democrat. "When Pinochet's rule ends, the right in Chile will be thoroughly discredited," he predicts. But, he adds, "it has excellent prospects for an early recuperation."

From the point of view of the right, not very much good has happened in Chilean politics since 1938, when a Popular Front government took office. Between that point and the election of Salvador Allende in 1970, only one elected administration (that of Jorge Alessandri, in 1958–64) could be regarded as more or less congenial to its interests; every other was committed to change in some sense or another. Even that of Carlos Ibáñez del Campo (1952–58), though conservative on economic policy generally, was responsible for a suffrage reform that enfranchised thousands of Chilean rural laborers, setting the stage for a profound alteration in the composition of the electorate.

The result has been that since 1938, the Chilean business and landowning elite has gradually withdrawn from active political life, because of its inability to compete successfully among the ever-increasing variety of participants. Conservative parties and politicians, of course, remained active in national life to the very end of the democratic period, convinced that the pendulum would eventually swing back in their direction (as, in fact, it almost did in 1970, and again in 1972–73). At the same time, parliamentary life offered the right repeated opportunities for obstruction, obfuscation, delay, or merely vengeance (sometimes working hand-in-glove with Marxist parties against the reformist center). On the other hand, the right in Chile cannot quite overcome a certain evident ambivalence toward democratic institutions—particularly the economic right, which remembers all recent governments prior to Pinochet's as fundamentally unfriendly and therefore is unenthusiastic about returning to a system that would resemble the one in force before 1973.

Though there is much talk in conservative circles in Chile about "another Allende," or returning to the "chaos of the Popular Unity period," the Christian Democrats are viewed

with equal distrust. It was, in fact, the land and tax reforms of
President Eduardo Frei (1964–70), that drove Chilean conservatives to one last effort to regain control of the presidency in
1970. Former President Jorge Alessandri was, so to speak,
resurrected as their standard-bearer; the principal target was
the Christian Democratic candidate selected to succeed Frei,
Radomiro Tomic. The unintended beneficiary was Salvador
Allende, whose candidacy the right had seriously underestimated, just as it had overestimated Alessandri's possibilities
of recapturing the presidency.

The Allende period (1970–73) was more traumatic still,
confirming the notion, already widespread among the Chilean
right, that democracy inevitably meant ever more exaggerated
expressions of radical populism and, with them, disorder and
the eventual threat of a Marxist putsch. Thus, while the
Christian Democrats and other parties of the center were at
the very beginning willing to work with Allende, the right
started sounding out army officers about a coup the morning
after his election. (Had Allende proceeded differently, of
course, these efforts would never have borne fruit.)

The right greeted the coup of September 1973 with frank
elation; it eagerly collaborated with the military government
in every way possible, and acted as the principal civilian
mouthpiece and apologist at home and abroad. Since 1983,
however, it has been divided between what might be called
"political" and "antipolitical" wings. The latter is the larger of
the two, including the near totality of the business and
landholding communities. Its views might be summarized in
the formula "Chile is not yet ready for democracy," which is
another way of saying that Chileans cannot be trusted not to
repeat the experience of 1964–73 and therefore should be kept
in some kind of permanent political tutelage, such as pre-
scribed in Pinochet's 1980 Constitution. This charter basically
establishes a truncated form of representative government in
which a popularly elected lower house of parliament will be
under the constantly restraining influence of an authoritarian
president and the military-dominated National Security
Council. On paper this system appears to be a compromise

between the old (pre-1973) political order and the new (1973–88); how it will work in practice, however, remains to be seen.

The political wing of the right is a mixed bag of politicians and intellectuals, many of whom were politically active before 1973 and favor a full return to normal democratic institutions. The most easily identifiable component is the old National party, successor to the Conservatives and Liberals—the parties that dominated Chilean politics in the interwar period. The Nationals were active in the opposition to both the Frei and the Allende administrations, and since 1985 they have operated as a quasi-opposition force against Pinochet. The party has experienced a number of splits and crises of leadership since then, and there is serious doubt that it continues to represent a viable political force. On the other hand, it does continue to attract a fair number of experienced politicians with good contacts across the spectrum, often formed through marriage or other family ties.

One way of dividing the political and antipolitical right is according to who signed (with parties of the center and democratic left) the National Accord for a Transition to Full Democracy in 1985. The matter is not so simple, however, since the new National Renewal party contains people identified with both lines. Some, like the Nationals, have concluded that whatever the dangers and risks of democracy, it still offers over the longer term the best chance of preserving private property, civility, and internal concord— and of fending off any serious challenge from the revolutionary left. Others, particularly in National Renewal, had hoped to act as a "military party" for the armed forces, providing the personnel, and perhaps even the presidential candidate, in a government to emerge from the coming plebiscite.

This option is no longer viable, since in 1988 National Renewal—a union of three small parties—split into its original components.[3] Chile thus enters the next phase of its political life without a major organized political force on the right, either for or against the government. This circumstance bodes ill for the country's future, if for no other reason than that the decision to surrender power to civilians is one that can be made, sooner or later, only by the armed forces. They, in turn, have shown little disposition to deal with anyone but the right; they trust no one else, and will probably heed the counsel of no one else. Most sophisticated politicians of the center and left fully recognize this fact. But that does not necessarily resolve the question of precisely who is their proper interlocutor on the right, much less how that party or parties can be mobilized successfully toward a common goal.

The Left: Which Left?

Like the right, the left in Chile is more than it at first appears. In the past, the heart of the left's electoral forces were the Socialist and Communist parties, each resting upon a ready-made constituency of blue- and white-collar unions. In addition, the left appealed to the "progressive" fringes of the parties of the center and to a wide range of "independents"— office workers, professionals, artists, teachers, social workers, even a few members of the clergy. Indeed, before 1973 virtually anything that passed for avant-garde culture in Chile, and much connected with serious art, was in some ways vaguely or explicitly connected with the left. It is not surprising, for example, that both of Chile's Nobel laureates for literature, Gabriela Mistral and Pablo Neruda, have been associated with the Socialist and Communist parties; Neruda even served as a Communist member of the Chilean Senate for several years, and was the party's candidate for the presidency in 1969, until an alliance with other parties produced Salvador Allende.

One must also count among the left those forces that have never displayed a particular interest in parliamentary or electoral politics—action groups committed to violence, sabotage, and terrorism. These have been active since the late 1960s, and are today engaged in open warfare against the military regime. In the environment of stalemate that characterizes so much of Chilean politics, they provide the shock troops for a truly revolutionary policy, both for those who favor such and for those who merely wish to persuade the military to withdraw from power before it is too late. Before the coup, they included the Movement of the Revolutionary Left (MIR) and such smaller formations as the Organized Vanguard of the People (VOP), which assassinated a former Christian Democratic minister in 1971; today they also encompass the Manuel Rodríguez Patriotic Front (FPMR), which works hand-in-glove with the Communists and, in spite of denials, is probably their terrorist wing.

Since no elections have been held in Chile since 1973, it is difficult to say precisely how strong the left really is. There is no single party to which this end of the spectrum owes its loyalty; there are serious tactical and philosophical divisions within parties, complicated by the fact that both the Socialists and the Communists have people in exile as well as operating within the country. Public opinion polls confirm only broad tendencies—such as that approximately a third of the potential electorate continues to identify itself as such.[4] In addition, the internationalization of Chilean politics since 1973 has led to the introduction of heavy external financing, from Western Europe for the Socialists, and from Cuba and the Eastern bloc (but also some Western European parties and unions) for the Communists. Thus, some forces seem stronger on the ground than they may in fact be, but since the same phenomenon occurs among parties of the center, perhaps the problem is self-neutralizing. There is really no way to know.

Before 1970 it was common to say that the difference between the Socialists and the Communists was that the latter had accepted, both implicitly and explicitly, the constraints of the democratic system. Meanwhile, the Socialists were divided between revolutionary Marxists (who worked more or less in tandem with the violent left), Social Democrats, and people like Salvador Allende, who believed that it was somehow possible to combine or reconcile the two visions. Another way of contrasting the two was to point out that the Chilean Socialists were a truly national party, while the Communists were (and are still) one of the parties outside the Eastern bloc most firmly loyal to the Soviet Union. What the Communists have thought and done in Chile has, in any event, been easy to interpret within the wider logic of Soviet international policy. The twists and turns of Socialist conduct have been possible to understand only within the complicated context of Chilean politics itself.

The Socialist-Communist alliance dates to the late 1930s, but has never been an easy one. There always were serious differences of strategy and tactics, and these differences increased perceptibly during the 1960s, largely because of the example of the Cuban Revolution. Basically, the Communists sought to build coalitions with non-Marxist parties, thus enhancing the chances of success at the ballot box, while the Socialists feared that such arrangements would undermine the revolutionary purity of whatever government might emerge. In fact, both proved right. But neither realized until September 1970 that they might be called upon to apply both strategies simultaneously. Thus the very conditions that made possible Allende's election prevented him from governing effectively and coherently, since his own party refused to accept the kinds of restraints necessary to sustain him politically.

One way of sorting out the present state of the Chilean left is to examine what lessons it draws from the failure of the Allende experiment. Until 1980, the division went something like this: both the Communists and the right wing of the Socialist party held that the collapse of the government was caused by the left wing of the Socialists and their allies in the violent left, who frightened needlessly those sectors of the public that could easily have been neutralized or won over, and made impossible the kind of arrangement with the Christian Democrats that would have preserved democratic institutions, if not the Popular Unity program itself.

For its part, the revolutionary left—the insurgent wing of the Socialists and those elements of the MIR that survived the coup—argued that Allende failed because he temporized with his critics, failed to purge the armed forces of disloyal officers, and refused to arm and organize worker militias for the inevitable confrontation with the bourgeois order. In short, a serious Trotskyist-Leninist appraisal.

The difference in historiographic schools reflects the continuing division of the Chilean left into democratic and nondemocratic traditions, but only to a point. The Communists are obviously not a democratic party, even though they functioned as such within the Chilean political system for many years. This anomaly was due as much as anything to the unique opportunities for participation that the local environment offered, but also to a strong Soviet interest in a model for Eurocommunism that would be convincing in more central political theaters, where the stakes were notably higher than in far-off Chile. (The fact that the Allende government was taken so seriously by people in Italy, France, and Spain suggests that this notion was by no means frivolous.)

In addition, by placing the blame for failure on the left wing of the Socialist party and the MIR, the Communists were settling old scores with forces that continually refused to subordinate themselves to the party's direction and often sabotaged its best efforts to consolidate the Allende regime. Even in defeat, the Communists could thus be shown to have been right all along—all the more persuasively, since, as in the case of the Spanish civil war, in narrow strategic terms they certainly were.

Today it is far more difficult to know what all of this means for Chile's political future. Since 1980, the Communists have shifted their own tactical and strategic appreciation of the situation, and have embraced the slogan "Destroy the dictatorship by any means necessary." The party claims that this is not a sudden embrace of the "violent road to power," which it so long opposed, but merely a tactical adjustment to changing circumstances. However, one cannot help noting that there has been a serious realignment on the left, and the Communists have now been brought together with former rivals and adversaries—the leftmost wing of the Socialists, under Clodomiro Almeyda, and the MIR. Together these three elements constitute the United Left (formerly the Popular Democratic Movement).

This leaves the rest of the Socialist party split into three or four groups, all of which accept a social democratic synthesis of Marxist economic and political doctrine. The most important, led by Carlos Núñez, joined with other parties, including two on the right, in signing the National Accord, while the Communists and their allies chose to remain outside it. Since 1987, the United Left has incorporated not merely the *violentista* wing of Chilean Marxism, but the Christian Left, MAPU, and even the Radical party, an affiliate of the Socialist International. Does this mean that the Communists and Almeyda Socialists have abandoned violence? Or that the Christian Left, MAPU, and the Radicals have embraced it? The answer to both is probably no; the tactical and philosophical boundaries between democratic and nondemocratic left simply are continuing to shift.

This is a serious problem for Chile's future, since if politics as usual is ever to resume, there must also be some kind of substantial force on the left that unhesitatingly accepts democratic pluralism and is seen to do so by those who choose not to vote for it. It is also true, however, that some place must eventually be made for the Communist party, which will not disappear, regardless of all efforts by the present regime and Constitution to outlaw it.

It remains to be seen whether the Communists will easily consent to play the role that other forces in Chilean politics find it convenient for them to play. A "domesticated" Communism is necessary to the Socialists, since if they are eventually to replicate the success of their colleagues in France, Spain, Portugal, and Italy, they must have something to their left to which they can pose a credible democratic alternative. (The same is true for those Socialists who dream of reviving the kind of Socialist-Communist alliance that brought Allende to power.)

The center also needs the Communists to resume their historic role as a quasi-bourgeois parliamentary party, both because it believes that having them inside the system (and therefore constrained by it) is better than not and (what amounts to the same thing) because it wishes to reconstitute the political game as it existed prior to 1970. The problem is rendered even more difficult by the Constitution of 1980, whose Article 8 declares it unconstitutional to propagate doctrines that promote violence, a totalitarian conception of society, or a society based on the class struggle. Even more importantly, the armed forces have made it clear on repeated occasions that they will not countenance the reappearance of Communism in Chilean politics.

Evidently, the matter will have to be resolved in two distinct phases. First, the armed forces must be persuaded to allow the right, the center, and the democratic left to reconstitute a representative political system. Then, following the example of Spain, the Communist party must be legalized and reintegrated into the political game by an early civilian government.

It is difficult to see how this can be managed in a neat and clear-cut fashion. In the first place, the Communists themselves, well aware of the devastating effects this scenario has had on their Spanish counterparts, may have no particular interest in playing their assigned role. Second, the armed forces too are aware of the probable outcome—the survival of Communism in a domesticated "political" form; harmless or even laudable as this may seem to outsiders, it runs counter to the military's view of the nation's future. Third, no one can be certain that—even if the Communists can be encouraged to publicly disavow violence and sever their obvious connection with the terrorist left—they would be acting in good faith. The discovery in 1986 of huge arms caches in northern Chile raised serious doubts even among some elements of the democratic opposition who most want to believe that the Communists were forced into their present intransigent position rather than that they more or less freely chose it.

Finally, the line between democratic and nondemocratic left in Chile can never be as neat as many Chileans (and Americans) might desire. Such a division is a technical impossibility because of old traditions, friendships, and family relations, and the experience of shared suffering at the hands of an enemy that recognizes no difference between Social Democracy and Communism, much less a Marxism that is intellectual rather than operational. It is said that on both sides of the divide there are people who favor the violent road and others who desire a peaceful approach, but the degree to which one or the other group prevails may depend in the long run on what opportunities are offered by the concrete situation.

Unfortunately, the general trend of conduct by the Pinochet regime tends to strengthen the most irresponsible and violent elements of the left; and the conduct of the army and police, particularly in the poor neighborhoods that ring Santiago, tends to refresh periodically the ranks of the MIR and other terrorist movements. On the other hand, Communists appear to be under considerable pressure from some of their rank and file to take a more "participatory" role in politics; though the party earlier declared its intention to boycott the plebiscite, now that the prospect of a Pinochet defeat seems possible, it is suddenly suggesting that it would interpose no obstacles to those of its members who might wish to vote no.

Finding the Center

Opinion polls demonstrate repeatedly that the center is the strongest political tendency in Chile—stronger, in fact, than ever before. Of this tendency, the Christian Democrats are evidently the strongest group; the latest surveys show that the party commands the support of 41 percent of the potential electorate[5]—not a majority, but infinitely closer to it than any other conceivable centrist alternative.

Between 1938 and 1958 the most important party of the center was the Radicals, who have since been gradually replaced by the Christian Democrats. The role of the Radical party was really not so much to represent a force of populist aggregation, but rather to take fullest advantage of its location at the crucial midpoint of the political spectrum. The Radicals were the "swing party," which made or unmade governments before 1958; in fact, it was hard to imagine any administration in which they would not play a major, or even decisive, role.

The case of the Christian Democrats is a bit different. Founded as a breakaway from the youth wing of the Conservative party in the years before World War II, this party entertained serious notions of becoming a true majority party, largely by appealing to newer elements of the electorate, particularly women, peasants, and shantytown dwellers in Chilean cities. By uniting some traditional themes (authority, austerity, commitment to legal procedures) with newer notions (land reform, self-management, economic nationalism), the Christian Democrats became the largest party in the country in the 1960s. In the process they pushed the Radicals into schism and near oblivion.

The election of a Christian Democratic president by overwhelming majority vote in 1964 would seem to have ratified the party's fundamental ambition. However, this was so only in appearance, since the crucial sixteen or so percentage points that put Eduardo Frei well over the 50 percent mark came from the right, whose parties chose not to run a candidate that year, and for whom the Christian Democrats were merely the lesser of two evils (the other being Salvador Allende, of the Socialist-Communist alliance). Once Frei began to govern, members of Congress from the right often joined with those from the left to block his initiatives. Furthermore, so bitter was the right over certain Christian Democratic policies, particularly land and tax reforms, that—as noted above—it chose to run a candidate of its own in 1970, splitting the votes of the center and right in such a way as to make possible by a hair the victory of Salvador Allende, the candidate of the left.

Even during Frei's presidency, however, the Christian Democrats were sharply divided among themselves. An insurgent left wing objected to many policies—particularly the failure to clearly demarcate a "noncapitalist" road to Chilean development—and while President Frei himself was the greatest asset to his party's right, he could not succeed himself, and there was no obvious personality to represent his

views. Thus, by 1970 some elements of the left wing of
Christian Democracy had split off to form MAPU, which
supported Allende, while the official candidate himself,
Radomiro Tomic, campaigned on a platform more radical than
that of his Socialist opponent.

Meanwhile, some voters on the rightmost fringes of
Christian Democracy probably deserted their party altogether
to vote for Alessandri. Indeed, were it not for the polarizing
policies of the Allende government (1970–73), the Christian
Democrats might well have gone the way of the Radicals. As
it was, the Popular Unity experiment pushed the Christian
Democrats strongly rightward and into an explicit alliance
with the National party. In the last congressional election, in
March 1973, the combined center-right list won almost
precisely the same percentage of the vote that had carried Frei
into office in 1964. This was a sign of intense opposition to
Allende and his programs, but not of any consensus on how
the country was to be governed.

After the coup on September 11, 1973, the military regime
quickly shattered this marriage of convenience. The Christian
Democrats are still the largest party in the country, but they
stand far from representing an absolute majority and have
rather problematic prospects of achieving one. A repetition of
1964—that is, some sort of coalition with the right—is not in
view; most of the elements on that end of the spectrum have
lost their enthusiasm for the democratic system altogether and
prefer to place their destiny in the hands of the armed forces.
There are one or two small parties—the larger of which is the
National party—that dissent from the views of their ideological cohorts and would in fact probably work with the
Christian Democrats in some sort of center-right coalition.

Moreover, fifteen years of military government have had
the effect of artificially enhancing the importance of the left,
to the point that almost any party of the center must
contemplate a coalition with it. This fact explains why it is so
important to know who on the left is, and who is not,
committed to returning to the rules of the game as it was
played prior to 1970. It also creates an obstacle to any kind of

understanding between the military and the Christian Democrats. If one considers the situation as it is today, common sense would seem to dictate that the Christian Democrats seek an understanding with the right, reassure the armed forces, and see what better days might bring. So far this has not happened, though it yet might. Conceivably, such a move could, however, provoke a schism, in which the party's left would leave en masse to join the United Left. On the other hand, if such an arrangement could be made with the tacit approval of the Núñez Socialists, it is perfectly possible.

There are, of course, other parties grouped around the center that are large enough to deprive the Christian Democrats of a wholly controlling role; but not a single one is significant enough to challenge them, including the Radicals and Social Democrats. There is probably also a significant portion of opinion, not identified with any party, that considers itself to belong to the center but is still waiting for some synthesis it can wholeheartedly support.

This dilemma explains the extraordinary role played in recent years in Chile by the Roman Catholic church. Always considered one of the more liberal or progressive ecclesiastical bodies in Latin America, the Chilean church has undertaken the specifically political task of brokering an understanding between all democratic forces and of mediating between them and the government. This explains the creation of the National Accord and the crucial role played by its coordinator, Sergio Molina, selected for this task by Cardinal Juan Francisco Fresno, the head of the Roman Catholic church in Chile.

There are real limits, however, to the role the church can play. It can create the minimum basis for a practical understanding between parties, but it cannot—in fact, does not try to—create a viable governing coalition. Also, since the government refuses to accept the mediation of the church in political matters, the latter has nowhere to go. Having been shown incapable of delivering results, it has been unable to prevent the Accord from fraying at its left and right edges. In addition, the church has problems of its own with insurgent priests and one particular bishop sympathetic to the violent left. The April 1987 visit of the Pope to Chile was supposed to address all these political and institutional matters, but it could not so easily reverse powerful trends that have been at work for years now. To the extent that they exist, however, these tendencies further complicate relations between church and state, or rather, between the church and the armed forces. They severely limit the church's scope of possible maneuver and its capacity to seriously engage the military government.

The Abiding Military

The armed forces of Chile are both the problem and the solution to the nation's dilemma. To state the matter baldly, the principal base of support for the Pinochet regime is its control and support of the military establishment and police, and any attempt to bring about a democratic transition requires their assent and even active participation. While some within the high command—particularly in the navy and air force—are known to be uncomfortable with the increasing personalization of the regime, and above all with Pinochet's plan to extend his rule eight and perhaps even sixteen years, the one truly essential and dominant branch of the service, the army, is firmly in the dictator's camp. As long as that is so, no change in political institutions can be initiated by—much less win acceptance among—the armed forces as a whole.

Three obstacles stand in the way of a serious understanding between the military and the political class. The first is sociological: Until the 1970s the military was seriously underpaid and enjoyed declining social prestige in what was, after all, the most civilian of Latin American political cultures. Since the coup, the size of the armed forces has been notably increased, as have been pay, allowances, perquisites, and social prestige. The wives of high-ranking officers are now received in social circles in Santiago that would have been all but inaccessible to them before 1973. How a future civilian government will approach this matter remains to be seen, but the evidence from the past is not very encouraging. It was

under the Christian Democrats (1964–70), in fact, that both
military spending and allocations for pay and allowances
declined most sharply, and for the left, quite understandably,
the military as an institution has become something of a bete
noire.

The second obstacle, which is political, is closely related to
the first. The known fact that all branches of the armed forces
perpetrated serious human rights violations after the coup—
and, indeed, have done so sporadically in the years since
then—raises their understandable concern that a return to
democratic institutions and the rule of law will usher in a
series of investigations and trials, in which both active and
retired officers would be dishonored and punished. Such have
already taken place across the border in Argentina, where
even under circumstances far more favorable to the new
government than are likely to prevail in Chile, it has been
necessary to compromise on matters of judicial principle and
legal fact.

While one could argue that the Argentine armed forces
have come out of their dilemma more comfortably than many
might have expected (or wished), in Chile the signs point to
the reverse outcome. The fact that such trials have been held
at all—and that a handful of serving flag officers has been
condemned, cashiered, and imprisoned—represents a mortal
threat that must be resisted at all costs. Though the National
Accord specifically sought to reassure the armed forces on this
point, it is difficult to believe that promises made now will be
possible to keep once the political context has greatly
changed. Meanwhile, General Pinochet plays upon the fear of
his officers whenever other forms of persuasion seem to be
failing. And, of course, the longer the regime remains in
power, the more incidents are bound to occur that underline
its basic illegitimacy and enrich the potential docket of any
future court of review.

Finally, there is a marked ideological distaste on the part of
most Chilean officers for what democracy in their country
historically meant. From this follows a visceral reluctance to
turn power over to the political class, even in the absence of

the disincentives outlined above. To be sure, certain kinds of politicians might in theory be acceptable to the military establishment—former Senator (and former Interior Minister) Sergio Onofre Jarpa, or former Foreign Minister Hernán Cubillos. It is even possible to imagine circumstances under which a right-wing Christian Democrat, such as former Senator Juan Hamilton, would win approval.

The choice, however, is that of the armed forces only in the first instance. Jarpa could never win an open election, and Hamilton has already been rejected twice for the leadership of his own party. Nor is there any way of guaranteeing that even if one or the other were to serve a full presidential term (or a version thereof, shortened for purposes of transition), he would be succeeded by someone equally palatable to the military. Again, the Spanish metaphor, while reassuring to many moderates, suggests an almost inevitable move in the direction of socialism once the restraints of the old regime are fully lifted—or, even if not that, certainly some form of populism that many in the military find equally distasteful. Any politician or diplomat who attempts to convince the military that this cannot happen is promising something no one can deliver.

Perhaps, however, the real link that binds the military to Pinochet is fear of the unknown. At some level, many officers doubtless recognize that their corporate interests are bound to suffer over the long run if some means is not found to withdraw gracefully from the political scene. On the other hand, since no obvious painless solution seems to be at hand, it is easier simply to postpone matters until a day "when conditions are ripe." This alternative is precisely what the Constitution of 1980 provides: a quasi-legal means of postponing harsh political realities indefinitely, while Pinochet and the civilian groups that support him do less than nothing to prepare the way for an eventual transition. The military, of course, cannot be expected to design long-range political solutions for Chile, but as long as no one can offer it one, it is bound to take the path of least resistance.

Paths to a Solution

Perhaps the best way of summarizing this discussion is to note that Chile's political dilemma is really one of sharply conflicting agendas for the future. The right would like to turn the clock back to the mid-1930s or before, but, knowing that this is impossible, prefers military rule. The small group of conservative politicians who, for reasons of opportunism, self-criticism, or genuine democratic conviction, has decided that a return to representative institutions serves their purposes better in the ultimate instance, represents neither a large enough or powerful enough segment of the right to convince the armed forces to break with Pinochet, nor a meaningful enough chunk of conservative opinion to effectively broker a transition between the military and other political forces.

Two quite different scenarios dominate the agenda of the left. For the moderate wing of the Socialist party, and perhaps MAPU and the Christian Left, the ideal outcome would be a situation in which, ultimately, many of the themes of the Allende experiment could be resumed, this time with the benefit of hindsight, self-criticism, even a genuine commitment to democracy and the rule of law. Many of these constituents recognize that socialism is not a likely prospect for the near term, but regard the reestablishment of democratic institutions as a necessary precondition and, even more than that, as a positive good in and of itself. It is difficult to see what these people can do to convince the military and the right that this, and not something else, is their purpose, particularly when the division between the moderate and revolutionary left is so difficult to demarcate.

For the revolutionary left—the Communists, the MIR, the Almeyda Socialists—the near-term goal is to destabilize the military regime. They are confident that sooner or later the context will be favorable to "deep democratic changes" of a type not yet seen in Chile—that is, a full-blown revolutionary state of the kind found in Cuba or Nicaragua. This wing of the left has no particular interest in designing negotiated solutions, but rather expects to benefit either from the lack of them or from the emergence of a weak democratic successor to Pinochet. It thus has no responsibility to outline a viable path to transition, and no obligation to subscribe to one devised by others. Yet precisely because it commands the most disciplined and best-organized force in the opposition, it is a factor that both the democratic left and the center cannot ignore. And to the extent that either appears to be working, or even contemplating working, with this sector, crucial doubts will be raised in the high command of the armed forces.

For the Christian Democrats, evidently, the ideal solution would be a new Christian Democratic government, or a coalition in which they would be the most important member. From a theoretical point of view this makes sense, given the party's size and location on the political spectrum, and because in a very general way its basic values are consubstantial with those of most Chileans. In terms of overall policy this solution would probably represent a resumption of the Frei administration—subject, presumably, to the same internal stresses, whether within the party or between it and any coalition partner. It is fruitless to speculate on how successful a replay of the earlier Christian Democrat period would be, since the only combination of which the military could possibly approve would be a coalition between the party's more conservative wing and the right. This, in turn, would require a whole host of tacit understandings between the Christian Democrats, the left, and the right—a prospect which is hardly yet in sight.

For the armed forces and their civilian supporters, the problem is how to get all of the political elements in Chile to accept the rules established by the Constitution of 1980—a kind of judicial straitjacket intended to reassure the military that nothing like the Allende regime will ever again occur. However, only a tiny minority of politicians—basically those who support the regime openly—can feel comfortable operating with its restraints. Consequently, whereas it is true that the opposition may disagree on the nature of the post-Pinochet political order, the government and the armed forces insist upon imposing one that is unnatural and unworkable.

Theoretically, the charter could be accepted as a basis for discussion, but only with the more or less explicit understanding that it will be altered and rendered more flexible at the earliest possible date. So far the armed forces have not shown a willingness to consider this possibility. Thus, if there is to be a solution in Chile, something must give—one of the walls that currently divide the different elements of civil society must collapse and open the possibility of new political combinations. The military must take matters into its own hands and, overruling its nominal leaders, initiate serious conversations with a broad spectrum of the opposition, such as occurred in Portugal in 1974. Or the Christian Democrats and other forces of the center must reach an understanding with the right that will offer the armed forces an alternative sufficiently attractive to act upon. Or the right must make a clean break with Pinochet and accept an unambiguous partnership with the center and democratic left, depriving the regime of its last reserves of political and ideological (as well as technical) support.

None of these alternatives lies immediately within view. But neither does the notion of "revolution from below"— massive demonstrations, strikes, or acts of terrorism that would make the country ungovernable and therefore, presumably, convince the military to relinquish power under the most unfavorable of circumstances. Nor is it possible to pretend that Chilean politics do not exist, and simply to allow another eight or sixteen years of rule that will be much the same as the past fifteen.

Today most of the hopes of the opposition are focused on a no vote in the upcoming plebiscite, in which Pinochet is overwhelmingly expected to be the government candidate. While the present dictator is the strongest of all possible proregime candidates, he is also the weakest—that is, he is the logical and irresistible target for all those who oppose the government. Thus, his defeat is almost certain if the contest is free and open, and the results faithfully recorded. Such a defeat would be devastating psychologically to the regime, and to Pinochet personally, but would not immediately solve the country's political problems.

Even if Pinochet manages to win the plebiscite (through fraud, intimidation, incomplete voter registration, low participation, or an unexpected backlash against the opposition), the legitimacy of his regime will not be significantly enhanced. In the best of cases, without massive and evident fraud, he cannot hope to win by a margin large enough to be interpreted as a mandate—particularly for eight more years of dictatorship. Nor will the opposition have any interest in attesting to the purity of the process if Pinochet somehow succeeds.

The dictator's supporters seem not to have thought these problems through. Instead, they imagine that the prospect of elections for a new Congress in 1990 (one with few powers, and from which the left evidently will be excluded) will divert the attention of the opposition for a time, and that somehow Pinochet and his most moderate opponents will learn to live together in the 1990s—he as a civilian chief of state (but with the full support of the military),[6] the opposition as a talking shop with no capacity to alter the system or to circumscribe the powers of the president. As for the left, these people hope that in time it will simply disappear as a political power.

This scenario is wildly unrealistic, but Pinochet and his supporters sincerely believe in it—and, in truth, given the alternatives, they have no choice but to do so—either that, or precipitously alter the rules of the game altogether. The only certainty, therefore, is that the political stakes in Chile during the next few months and years will be very high, with the possibilities of victory for any side circumscribed by history, politics, and the fears that the government and opposition continue to harbor against each other.

One must hope that the right combination of pragmatism, trust, and common sense on the part of all parties will somehow prevail, so that Chile can rejoin the community of Western nations, in which it once occupied so distinctive a place.

Notes

1. That is, according to the Constitution of 1980, whose permanent (as opposed to transitional) articles will come into full effect after 1989.

2. A variant of this scenario suggested earlier this year by the air force member of the junta, General Fernando Matthei, would substitute competitive elections for an up-or-down vote. The assumption is that if the center, right, and left (or even merely the center and left) each fielded a candidate, Pinochet might win by a small plurality. Implementing this plan would require amending the Constitution of 1980, and that can be accomplished only by plebiscite.

3. These were the Independent Democratic Union (UDI), led by Jaime Guzmán; the National Labor Front (FNT) of Sergio Onofre Jarpa; and the National Union Movement (MUN) of Andrés Allamand. Formed in 1986, National Renewal was an uneasy alliance, in which all three leaders thought of themselves as presidential possibilities—a view not widely shared, apparently, by the armed forces.

4. In a survey conducted by the Latin American Faculty of Social Sciences (FLACSO) in Santiago, Chile in May 1986, roughly 21 percent of respondents described themselves as adhering to the "center left," 13 percent to the "left." The issue is somewhat complicated by the fact that because most of the parties of the center—Christian Democrats, Radicals, Social Democrats—actually consider themselves center-left, they are competing for some of the same ideological space as the more moderate wing of the Socialist party. Nonetheless, it is reasonable to assume that in any future election the Socialist and Communist parties, in the event they were allowed to participate, would attain a combined total of at least a quarter and (together with other small parties, like MAPU [Movement of Unified Popular Action, a group which split off from Christian Democracy in 1969 and subsequently formed part of the Allende coalition in 1970–73] or the Christian Left) possibly even one-third. See Mark Falcoff, "Going to Extremes," *New Republic*, 7 September 1987, pp. 26–33.

5. Carlos Huneeus, *Los Chilenos y la Política: Cambio y Continuidad en el Autoritarismo* (Santiago: Centro de Estudios de la Realidad Contemporánea, 1987).

6. One argument frequently advanced by Chilean government spokespersons is that after 1989 the president will lack the transitional articles of the 1980 Constitution, which give dictatorial powers to Pinochet. This is true in the narrow technical sense. However, it is difficult to imagine that someone who has ruled as an absolute dictator for fifteen years will suddenly embrace a new governing style because of a legal technicality. To be sure, to violate his own Constitution would be a drastic step for Pinochet, but he has already betrayed one set of institutions—those to

which he took an oath of loyalty when commissioned in 1936. He could surely find excuses to betray yet another.

THE 1988–89 PLEBISCITE IN CHILE: POLITICAL SCENARIOS FOR THE FUTURE

Arturo Valenzuela

If the plebiscite is held, as seems likely, President Pinochet will probably be the candidate. He has substantial political skills, the right-wing parties seem incapable of uniting around an alternate candidate, and public opinion polls indicate that he has a core of broad-based support. The likely outcome of the plebiscite is that the no vote will be greater than the yes vote, since Chile's democratic tradition is generating growing resistance to continued authoritarian rule. Many Chileans have suffered economic hardship as well as political repression under Pinochet. If the yes vote wins, it would mean either that the election was fraudulent, or that the Chilean people were afraid of the unknown and decided that they were actually benefiting economically from Pinochet's rule. The democratic transition will be easier if Pinochet is defeated. Even then, the road will be rocky if the democratic opposition fails to unite around a single candidate. If the opposition fragments or if Pinochet wins the plebiscite, military intervention could ensue.

The years 1988 and 1989 are destined to be remembered as pivotal ones in contemporary Chilean history. According to the 1980 Constitution, the commanders in chief of the army, navy and air force and the director general of the national police must designate, on or before December 11, 1988, a candidate to occupy the country's presidency for an eight-year term beginning March 11, 1989. The nominee must be

29

ratified in a national plebiscite to be held no sooner than thirty days and no later than sixty after his name is officially announced. This means that the plebiscite could take place at any time up to February 2, 1989.[1]

Should the commanders not be able to agree on a nominee within forty-eight hours after convening for that purpose, the decision would revert to the National Security Council, which would choose a candidate by a majority vote. The National Security Council is constituted by the four commanders, the president of the republic, and the presidents of the Supreme Court and the Council of State. For this vote alone the comptroller general would also join the National Security Council.[2]

If the government candidate is defeated in the plebiscite, President Augusto Pinochet Ugarte's term and that of the military junta, made up of the three other commanders and an army representative appointed by Pinochet, would be extended for one year, after which competitive presidential elections and elections to the national Congress would be held. If the military nominee wins, he is required to call congressional elections nine months after he commences his term.[3]

It is no secret that President Pinochet, who came to power in the military coup that overthrew President Salvador Allende in September 1973, has every expectation of being nominated to succeed himself. In 1980, to the consternation of the members of the Council of State, Pinochet rejected the final draft of the Constitution submitted to him by the council's president, conservative former President Jorge Alessandri. The council's draft had proposed an end to military rule and open elections by 1985. Pinochet instructed his advisers to rewrite the pertinent transitional articles so that he could stay in office another sixteen years, for a grand total of twenty-four years at the helm of the nation. After considerable discussion, his advisers persuaded him that it would be difficult to obtain ratification of the document with such a provision, proposing instead a "midterm" plebiscite as a compromise formula, one clearly aimed at satisfying the president's wishes. Although the Constitution bars Chilean presidents from succeeding themselves, the transitional articles exempt Pinochet by name from that restriction.[4]

Pinochet and his advisers were confident in 1980 that a plebiscite in which the general was the only candidate could successfully be turned into a referendum on the government's performance. There was optimism in official circles that the Chilean economic model would succeed in producing a new third world miracle, rendering the old parties and ideologies obsolete and establishing Pinochet as the popular savior of the nation.[5] The ratification of the Constitution with a 67 percent approval rate in a national referendum only reinforced this view.[6]

The massive protests that broke out in 1983 shattered the regime's carefully structured plans. Opposition groups and political parties that even government opponents feared had been crushed came back to life. Few observers believed that Pinochet would be able to stay in office until 1989, let alone beyond. In 1984 and 1985 cabinet officers and junta members advocated constitutional reforms that would permit the election of a Congress and competitive presidential elections by 1989. However, Pinochet doggedly refused to accede to any changes in the constitutional itinerary and successfully weathered the storm of protests. Today few Chileans think that there will be an alternative to the plebiscite, or that Pinochet will make way for another candidate.

But the road for Pinochet and for Chile has not been easy and will not be easy in the coming months. The president will continue to have difficulty making a strong case to his military colleagues in the other services that he should be the nominee. He is a controversial and feared figure and has not been doing well in the public opinion polls. Whether or not he wins the nomination, it is uncertain that the official government candidate can win a majority of the vote for the yes option, raising serious doubts about the prospects for full implementation of the transition formula. And even if the plebiscite is held and the official candidate wins, Chile is likely to face growing political unrest and violence, calling into question the country's ability to return to stable democracy.

The objective of this chapter is to weigh the likelihood of different scenarios for regime transition in Chile and to speculate about the short-term and long-term consequences of each.[7] The first part will focus on the likelihood that the plebiscite will be held and that Pinochet will be the candidate. The second will consider the implications for Chile's transition process of either a victory or a defeat for the government nominee. Chart 1 summarizes the various scenarios and their respective probabilities.

1988 Scenarios—Plebiscite and Candidates

There are two broad scenarios possible in 1988. The less likely, with a 20 percent probability, is the cancellation of the plebiscite. That is, there is an 80 percent probability that the plebiscite will take place, either with or without Pinochet as the candidate.

Cancellation of the Plebiscite (20 Percent Probability)

Cancellation of the plebiscite is very unlikely because it would involve a departure from the procedures outlined in the Constitution. Because the Chilean armed forces feel strongly that the 1980 Constitution is their legacy to the nation and take very seriously the importance of strict adherence to legal norms and constitutional precepts, they would strongly resist any departure from the norms set forth in that document.[8]

Two factors might come together to build pressure for a cancellation of the plebiscite. The first would be a continued poor showing by the official candidate in all the polls, especially those commissioned by the government. The second would be a sharp outbreak of terrorist violence, including attacks aimed at innocent civilians. Neither of these factors alone would be sufficiently important to force a deviation from the government's transition timetable—but together they could create a climate of uncertainty that would

Chart 1.

CHILEAN SCENARIOS: ROUGH PROBABILITIES OF OUTCOMES

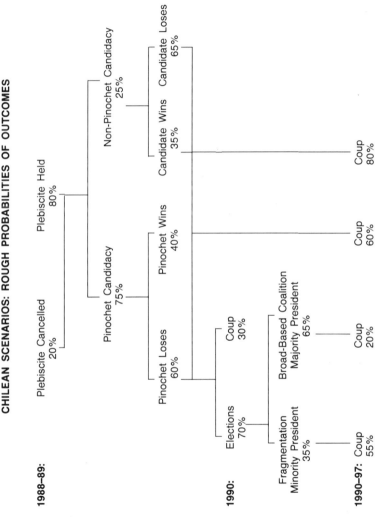

generate concern among the commanders in chief of the armed forces about losing control of the political process should the plebiscite proceed as scheduled. It is not out of the question that elements who support a continuation of authoritarian rule might deliberately provoke terrorist incidents if they perceived that the government was heading toward electoral defeat. Their work would be facilitated by revolutionary elements on the left committed to the doctrine of "popular war." The extensive infiltration of these groups by elements of the security forces makes it problematic to judge the degree to which terrorist incidents are provoked by enemies of the regime, or by some of its staunchest advocates.

Even in such a climate, it is difficult to imagine the cancellation of the plebiscite because it would violate the very constitutional precepts the government and the armed forces are so intent on upholding. The only realistic way for the plebiscite to be cancelled is for the junta to call a plebiscite to modify the Constitution and adopt an alternative procedure. Such a step would be lengthy, complicated, and difficult to undertake in a climate of violence and uncertainty. Even if there were substantial evidence that the government candidate might lose under the plebiscitary formula, the junta would more likely take a chance on a loss, which would lead to open elections within a year, than follow a path that threatens to upset what it sees as a carefully planned transition process. Further complicating the picture is the fate of General Pinochet. If a plebiscite were called cancelling the referendum on a government candidate and opening the way for free elections, Pinochet and his advisers might insist that the way be cleared for him to run in the open election—making the fate of the vote on the constitutional changes itself open to question.

Government Nominee for the Plebiscite: Pinochet (75 Percent Probability), Other (25 Percent Probability)

Although there is little doubt that the Chilean regime intends to carry out the plebiscite on schedule, it is not a foregone conclusion that Pinochet will be the candidate. In late 1985, the general was in serious trouble. In the aftermath of the signing of the National Accord for a Transition to a Full Democracy—a broad, multiparty pact whose signers range from moderate socialists to moderate rightists—most Chileans believed that Pinochet would be out of office after 1989. Opposition political leaders were hopeful that he would be forced to resign before the end of his term. And while prominent leaders of the political right and the business community argued forcefully that Pinochet should be permitted to remain in office until 1989 in order to provide for constitutional continuity, they clearly felt that it would be better for the country to depersonalize the transition process and choose another person for the next presidential term. Most, including at least two of the other commanders, found it logical to think that those who supported the regime and a continuation of its policies would benefit from a candidate who could appeal to supporters of the moderate opposition parties fearful of alliances with the Marxist left. A "Pinochetismo" without Pinochet would give those committed to the 1980 Constitution a better chance to see the Constitution implemented.[9]

Today, however, Pinochet has a 75 percent chance of being selected as the government nominee, once again overcoming widespread speculation that he was politically finished. This is due in part to the failure of the National Accord to produce a consensus among opposition forces.[10] The Accord collapsed because of profound disagreements between the parties of the right and those of the center. Rightist parties were not willing to accept an ongoing alliance with the center so long as the center continued to advocate mass mobilization and protests in consort with the left. Centrist parties in turn argued that it was illusory to believe that the armed forces would modify their itinerary without feeling the pressure of popular discontent—pressure that they felt had exacted the only real concessions the regime had provided. Pinochet and the authorities skillfully played on these disputes, raising fear among constituents of rightist parties that any alliance with opposition forces would mean a return to the situation that prevailed under the Popular Unity government.

More than any other factor, however, the passage of time has helped Pinochet's chances. As the plebiscite approaches, political leaders on the right, still committed to someone other than Pinochet in 1989, have been unable to muster the political courage or the requisite political strategy to propose a viable alternative candidate or candidates. The Chilean right is highly fragmented and disorganized—a collection of bickering personalities unable to unite in the face of a highly cohesive government and determined political leader. Everyone has expected that someone else would try to persuade the general to step down, and everyone has expected that someone else would propose alternative figures for consideration by the military commanders. In the final analysis, rightist political leaders have feared that their supporters would not agree to abandoning Pinochet or that their own political positions would be seriously undermined should the president actually be reelected.[11] Business leaders also have backed away from a suggestion that Pinochet be replaced, reflecting the reality of a private sector highly indebted to state-run financial institutions and subject to government decisions on a host of matters, ranging from subsidies to import regulations. Chilean government authorities have not hesitated to resort to direct economic pressures in an attempt to keep the business community loyal.

Pinochet's political skills have aided him in placing the leaders of the right in a position where they will be forced to accept his candidacy and become vocal supporters of his re-election. As early as 1986 he launched a vigorous campaign to convince the armed forces and his detractors on the right that he is fully prepared to take on the challenge of an electoral effort. He sharply increased his travel schedule, visiting remote communities, giving away public housing, and kissing babies, all under the close scrutiny of ubiquitous television crews. His skillful public relations staff embarked on an ambitious media campaign aimed at conveying in a reassuring and subtle way that Chileans now live in peace and prosperity, values that were "rescued" in the nick of time. Pinochet himself was no longer portrayed in military uniform with the stern look of a soldier, but in civilian dress with the smile of a kindly grandfather. He made it clear that government officials, including all of the country's governors and mayors (who are directly appointed by him), are charged with mobilizing support for the government in the electoral campaign, making ample use of state resources if necessary.[12]

The Comité Cívico was formed by prominent businessmen with a budget large enough to permit the publication of glossy literature and handsome lapel buttons. Its purpose was to galvanize the business community into supporting the "government candidate." A vast network of support in the business community could be counted on to generate newspaper and radio endorsements, and place additional pressure on private-sector firms to support the government. By the Chilean spring of 1987, the social, political, and economic pressure to get on the Pinochet bandwagon had extended into public and private agencies, universities, research institutions, and the mass media.[13]

The only hope for rightists and government officials keen on naming an alternative to Pinochet remained the continued low support for the president in most polls. As of August 1988, Pinochet's strength appeared to be no higher than 35 percent of the eligible population. This led some leaders on the right to think that Pinochet could be pressured into accepting another candidate if his standing in the polls did not improve.

However, for such a strategy to have a chance at success, its advocates would have to prove that alternative figures would do better than Pinochet in the plebiscite. In the absence of other publicly declared candidates, this task is impossible. Polling organizations have no way of determining the strength of unnamed candidates; what is more, phantom alternative candidates have no way of appealing to the public for support. Even if the polls show that Pinochet's support is weak, he can always argue that no one could do better than the man who has ruled Chile longer than anyone else in the nation's history.

Nor is it logical to assume that the Chilean military would ask Pinochet to step down in light of poll results. If civilian leaders of the Chilean right were reluctant to propose an alternative candidate for fear of displeasing Pinochet, military officers, particularly in the army, are much more vulnerable to the wrath of the army's commander in chief. Pinochet's dominance over the military, and the strong adherence to discipline and respect for hierarchy that characterizes the Chilean armed forces, make it virtually impossible to envision high-ranking officers challenging the president's wishes. There may be substantial concern in the armed forces that Pinochet's increased inability to separate his own personal fortunes from those of the country might be deleterious to the military as an institution over the long run, but no army officer could afford to take the first step and follow through on such worries without risking his career.

It is clear that General Fernando Matthei of the air force and Director General of the National Police Rodolfo Stange have had serious doubts about the wisdom of designating Pinochet for another term. Matthei has in private accused the government of attempting to have him dismissed from office through a rumor campaign involving his personal life. Both Matthei and Stange would probably vote for an alternative candidate if one were available. However, neither is powerful enough in his own right to suggest an alternative to Pinochet. Each is fully aware that Pinochet was able to remove Matthei's predecessor from the junta by conspiring with the other members. Admiral José Toribio Merino's position has often been ambiguous, but Toribio has always supported Pinochet in crucial showdowns, including the one with former junta member General Gustavo Leigh. None of the junta members has the force of personality, the vast resources of a complex state, or the access to intelligence and security forces that Pinochet has. What is more, Pinochet can use to his advantage the Constitution's provision calling for a unanimous vote on the nominee. If one or two of his colleagues hold out for another candidate, he can, as he has done before, invoke the ominous consequences any institutional split would have for the armed forces. He can also threaten to take the decision to the National Security Council, where he would most likely have the votes to impose his strategy.[14]

It is still conceivable that an alternative candidate could be chosen (25 percent probability). For this to occur, Pinochet would have to decide—on the basis of polls and his own political instincts—that he would be better off supporting an alternative candidate. If another candidate lost, Pinochet would avoid the humiliation of defeat and remain the most powerful man in the country. He would stay in office for a year until a new president was elected, then would retain his position as commander in chief of the army and serve as a lifelong member of the Senate.[15] Pinochet would also be a voting member of the National Security Council, a body empowered to review the decisions of all government institutions to ensure that their actions do not damage the nation's "institutionality" or otherwise "compromise its national security."[16]

Should the designated candidate win, he would owe his nomination and election to Pinochet, who would retain all of the posts enumerated above. As such, the new president would probably be a figurehead who was constantly second-guessed by his more powerful predecessor. However, the likelihood of an alternative candidate's winning is small (35 percent if such a candidate were nominated). While an alternative candidate might appeal to many middle-of-the-road voters interested in peace and continuity, he would not have enough time at this juncture to galvanize the forces of the government while distancing himself from Pinochet. At the same time, the candidate would be strongly rejected by most of the political opposition, including the Christian Democratic party. Such a candidate would threaten the prospects for a speedier transition to democracy and the hopes of opposition figures that the Pinochet era would soon come to an end through competitive elections. Opposition figures would be buoyed by Pinochet's withdrawal from the contest and determined to defeat the candidate in the plebiscite.

The scenario of an alternative candidate is improbable in the final analysis precisely because it depends on Pinochet's willingness to accept the idea that another individual should occupy the exalted niche he has carved for himself in Chilean history. It also depends on his ability to concede to his colleagues and himself that he might actually be defeated. All indications are that Pinochet would have a very hard time making such calculations. He has the pride of a soldier who is confident that he has never been defeated despite herculean odds. Close advisers to the general have noted that since the day of the coup, he has considered himself a marked man for having had the audacity to stand up to forces of international communism. The president can point to many instances in which both friends and enemies thought that he was politically finished, but his steadfastness and, in his view, divine intervention, helped him survive. He was virtually alone in insisting on the 1978 plebiscite that asked the country to support him in the face of human rights criticisms from abroad—a plebiscite he won. More dramatically, he survived the massive protest movements of 1983 and 1984 and the attempt on his life in September 1986, in which four of his bodyguards were killed.

Pinochet believes that he is indispensable to the nation— that he alone can guide Chile to win the battle against communist aggression from without and within. To give up at this point would be to run the risk of losing much that Pinochet believes he has accomplished. He has utter contempt for the political leaders who are fighting him, and believes that in the final analysis the people of Chile will choose him over a bickering lot of opportunists influenced by foreign money. And he has shown a ruthless determination to stop at nothing in attaining his objectives—including the forceful and illegal removal of junta colleague Air Force Commander Leigh in 1978 and the encouragement and protection of a secret police that has not stopped at Chile's borders in attempting to eliminate individuals viewed as threats to Pinochet's rule.[17]

Giving up the race would be an admission of weakness. Finally, individuals close to Pinochet say that he fears for the safety of his family and is convinced that he and they would be better off by staying in the presidential palace. Like Franco, whom he greatly admired, Pinochet at seventy-three believes that he should die in office at the service of his country.[18]

Plebiscite Outcome: Pinochet Win (40 Percent Probability), Loss (60 Percent Probability)

In assessing the possible outcomes of the plebiscite in Chile, we will assume that the candidate designated by the commanders in chief of the armed forces will be Pinochet. Although he will most likely gain the nomination, he stands a less than even chance of winning approval in the plebiscite (40 percent).[19] Public opinion polls rate him the least popular president in memory and suggest that he has less support than did former presidents Eduardo Frei and Salvador Allende at the most difficult junctures of their terms in office.

Pinochet as the government nominee will, however, significantly improve his chances of winning a fair election in the months ahead and reverse his low standing in the polls. The government will maintain its virtual monopoly control over television and has the undivided support of Chile's major private newspapers. Government publicity experts will openly appeal to middle-of-the-road Chileans by presenting the electoral option in dire terms as the plebiscite approaches, suggesting that a vote against Pinochet would be a vote for chaos and violence. Increases in terrorist activities would only help to reinforce that argument.[20]

At the same time, the increases in the price of copper and the continued inflow of foreign funds through international financial institution loans and the World Bank structural adjustment loan will give the government further resources to provoke a classic "political" business cycle. The housing program Pinochet has used as the cornerstone of his campaign was financed in part with large loans from the Inter-American Development Bank and the World Bank. Contingency plans prepared by government advisers have already designated additional domestic resources for public spending especially aimed at the poor. An important resource for the government is the vast network of social service agencies organized under the leadership of Lucia Pinochet, the president's wife. Furthermore, Chile's economy has not experienced the inflation and low growth rates of other Latin American economies, and the stabilization policies of the economic team led by Finance Minister Hernán Büchi have been praised as a model for developing countries.

While Pinochet and his advisers and supporters are banking on these factors to lead to a successful electoral outcome, and will indeed win over many Chileans who are fearful of the unknown, they are unlikely to overcome the deep-seated opposition to the regime among vast sectors of Chilean society. The country had a strong democratic tradition, and while many citizens welcomed the coup that ended the chaos and confrontation of the Allende years, the vast majority favor an immediate return to democracy.[21] Most politically active Chileans reject the legitimacy of the regime, and parties that at one time represented over 70 percent of the vote are actively supporting its end.[22]

At the same time, large numbers of less politically active citizens in Chile's working classes have suffered greatly during the fifteen years of military rule. Repeatedly local leaders have been arrested, mass raids in working-class neighborhoods have led to the humiliating detention of thousands of boys and men, and expressions of dissent have often been dealt with in brutal fashion. Social services for the poor, particularly medical care, have deteriorated substantially, unemployment rates have remained much higher than historic averages, and wage levels have not fully recovered, despite the improvement in the aggregate economic picture. The result has been that per capita consumption in Chile is only slightly better than it was in the late 1960s.[23] The situation today is vastly different from that in 1980, when Chile was awash with unprecedented consumer goods made possible in part by massive foreign borrowing. Today, the austerity plan designed to meet Chile's external obligations has meant a collective tightening of the belt that has affected low-income sectors more than others.[24]

Finally, the 1983 protest movement, which led to a massive outpouring of discontent with the Pinochet government, contributed to erasing much of the fear that Chileans still had, particularly in smaller and more rural communities. This means that far fewer Chileans will feel compelled to vote in favor of the government in the plebiscite because of fears that they would be identified and held accountable for their expression of dissent.

The only factor that might tip the scale in Pinochet's favor would be an unprecedented escalation of political violence. It is difficult to imagine such an escalation coming from the left. The Chilean Communist party has had to retreat from its advocacy of "all forms of struggle" in the face of widespread rejection of its policies from within its own ranks.[25] Though there are sectors in Chile that continue to advocate an escalation of violent confrontation, they are at present quite isolated, and it is doubtful whether they could generate the kind of violent outbreak that would be necessary for Pinochet to win the plebiscite.

The discussion so far has been premised on the assumption that the plebiscite will be conducted fairly. There is growing evidence that the 1980 plebiscite which ratified the Constitution was much more fraudulent than originally reported.[26] For a time, opposition figures feared that the government would ensure a favorable outcome for its cause by controlling the registration process. Pro-government supporters, including armed forces personnel, public employees, and government welfare recipients, were the first to register. The registration process was made unusually cumbersome by requiring that every citizen obtain a new identity card prior to registration and pay a fee that represented a hardship for poor Chileans. The insistence on a manual registration process rather than a computerized one linked to the national identity card was interpreted by many citizens as a deliberate attempt to restrict the size of the electorate in order to favor the government candidate.

Despite these difficulties, however, many more eligible voters registered than opposition leaders thought possible. By August 1988 it appeared that a figure of 6.5 million out of a total eligible population of approximately 8 million would be on the registration roles in time for the plebiscite. It appears that junta members were particularly insistent that a large enough population be registered to ensure the legitimacy of the vote.

It will be very difficult, however, for the government to significantly manipulate the results. The upcoming plebiscite will be conducted with a prior registration system, and the lists of those registered by polling stations will be open to opposition figures who wish to examine them. The election also will be monitored by poll watchers from each of the officially registered parties. At least three opposition parties will be able to designate poll watchers on a national level, decreasing the possibility of fraud during ballot counting. The election will be heavily monitored by local and international observers as well. In the most likely form of fraud, people would be excluded from voting places or found ineligible to vote in particular polling places on election day. However, if the opposition parties are vigilant, even such fraud would be difficult to perpetrate.

More than overt fraud in the voting or counting process, the election could be seriously tainted by various forms of intimidation. The experience of the internal elections of the conservative National Renewal party, held in March of 1988, suggests that government officials may use tactics of intimidation to encourage a yes vote. During that vote, municipal officials threatened citizens with job loss, removal from lists for new housing, and denial of permits to conduct business if they did not support the slate favored by the authorities. Local authorities could resort to similar tactics of intimidation in an attempt to maximize the vote for the government nominee.[27]

1988 and Beyond: Implications of the Plebiscite

Ironically, whether Pinochet wins or loses the plebiscite in a fair election, Chile faces a very difficult transition back to democracy. If the president wins, his supporters will hail the victory as a vindication of his rule, reinforcing the government's determination to stick closely to the 1980 Constitution. However, electoral victory for the government will be considered fraudulent by many Chileans and their foreign supporters. As many as 40 percent of the Chilean people consider the regime of General Pinochet fundamentally illegitimate. It is instructive that in a 1987 public opinion survey, a majority of respondents said they would not support the government in the plebiscite, but the same proportion were convinced that the government would engineer a win.[28]

Pinochet Victory in Plebiscite (40 Percent Probability)

Victory by the president and the prospect of another eight years of Pinochet leadership will only exacerbate political conflict. Many Chileans who retreated from protests and civil disobedience as the electoral contest grew closer will once again be tempted to join in efforts to overthrow or destabilize the regime. This applies to important sectors of the Christian Democratic party who have been strongly critical of the decision of party authorities to register their party in conformity with the regime's "parties" law.

A victory by Pinochet, particularly one that appears to be fraudulent, will only strengthen sectors of the extreme left who have argued that the only way the regime can be defeated is through armed struggle. It is no accident that the Communist party made its historic shift to support of armed insurrection after the approval of the 1980 Constitution, when it became apparent that the regime was achieving its aim of creating a new institutional order. More Chileans than before might be willing to risk harboring and supporting violent opponents of the regime, increasing the prospects for urban guerrilla warfare.[29]

Provisions in the Constitution and in junta laws banning all Marxist parties will only aggravate these tendencies by barring those parties and their leaders from active participation in political life, thereby forcing them to remain underground. In these circumstances, congressional elections in 1989 are unlikely to distract political elites into electoral campaigning, as the authorities hope they will, but will only heighten political tensions and confrontations.

At the same time, the governmental system outlined in the 1980 Constitution will not be accepted as legitimate by moderate political leaders. The Constitution is profoundly antidemocratic in several important respects. In addition to banning individuals from participation in political life because of their views, it envisions an all-powerful executive and a weak legislature, in which elected representatives could be sanctioned by nonelected bodies for introducing bills that are deemed subversive. The document calls for a permanent tutelary role for the armed forces through the National Security Council, which would be empowered to admonish elected officials if they are viewed as soft on issues of national security. It does away with popularly elected local government, which has been at the center of Chilean democracy for decades.

If the opposition decides to participate in parliamentary races and succeeds in gaining majorities in Congress, the weakness of the legislature vis-a-vis the president is a prescription for governmental paralysis. With few real powers and a president who is contemptuous of the political elites, the Congress would probably seek by all means possible to thwart executive authority.[30] Political stalemate and confrontation, with no resolution in sight until the presidential election of 1997, would undermine political governance and erode whatever democratic practices the country still had. It is thus likely that if Pinochet is elected, his term will be interrupted by another military coup (60 percent probability). The coup could be led by Pinochet himself and directed against the Congress or by someone else and aimed at deposing Pinochet if the armed forces perceived that the president was viewed as too old and controversial to continue his long rule of the country.[31]

Pinochet Defeat in Plebiscite (60 Percent Probability)

If Pinochet loses the plebiscite (60 percent probability), the prospects for transition to democracy will be better than if he wins. However, the process will not be easy, and Chile will face several months of political uncertainty and confrontation. The opposition groups will insist that the victory of the no vote is tantamount to a full rejection of the constitutional framework of the regime and will demand Pinochet's resignation, early open presidential elections, and the election of a Congress with constituent powers. They will insist on direct negotiations with the armed forces to implement these demands.[32] The government will argue that the defeat means simply that the itinerary set forth in the Constitution must be followed to the letter. This means that Pinochet would be president for another year, and elections for president and Congress would be held with all the restrictions delineated in the 1980 document. The armed forces are committed to this formula and will refuse to deal directly with the opposition. The climate of uncertainty will be aggravated by a weakening of the nation's economic picture as local businessmen attempt to transfer money abroad and foreign banks refuse to commit themselves to a restructuring of the foreign debt.

During the "year after the no," the prospect of another military coup led by high-ranking officers or Pinochet himself under the banner of a second Eleventh of September[33] is not out of the question (30 percent chance). A coup could result if an increasingly mobilized opposition's escalating demands for Pinochet's resignation and the transformation of the 1980 Constitution are accompanied by widespread repression and terrorist violence. Much, then, depends on the ability of moderate sectors within the opposition and the regime to work out an understanding for a mutual set of guarantees for the transition year. The opposition will have to set aside its desire to negotiate directly with the armed forces and be prepared to deal with Pinochet or his emissaries. In particular, it cannot expect to force Pinochet's resignation and should be prepared to accept the general outlines of the transition process described in the Constitution. Sectors in the Chilean political right and in the government should seek to guarantee a clean electoral contest and be prepared to consider drastic modifications of the emergency legislation still on the books. They also should seriously consider a constitutional amendment to be proposed by the junta that would reduce the number of nonelected members of the Senate and provide for an easier mechanism for constitutional change after the legislature is elected.

Independent of the ability of both parties to work out some basic guarantees for the electoral process, the conduct of the political opposition during the period prior to competitive elections and the "electoral options" it structures will have an important effect on the long-term success or failure of the transition process.

If the opposition is able to structure a common program and present a single candidate with a platform capable of satisfying the aspirations of Chileans across the political spectrum, while providing guarantees to the local and international business communities, it is likely to win with a majority of the votes on the first round of the open presidential race. Such an option, backed by the broad coalition of forces that formed the Democratic Alliance, along with additional sectors from the right, would most likely involve the selection of an independent candidate of the center right or a member of the right wing of the Christian Democratic party as standard bearer. This option depends on the ability of moderate socialists grouped in the Party for Democracy to hold their own in their competition with forces further to the left who are closer to the Communist party. With a decisive victory for the no vote, the moderate socialists would be significantly strengthened. This option has a 65 percent chance of success.

A second electoral option (35 percent probability) is one that would conform to the continued fragmentation of Chilean politics, which mirrors the tripartite options presented in the presidential election of 1973, in which Allende won with 36 percent of the vote. Under this scenario, the parties of the moderate left would disintegrate or opt for an alliance with the Marxist left, the Christian Democrats would proceed on their own with the expectation that they could win, and the right would structure its own party in the hopes of capturing the votes of the silent majority of Chileans grateful for the military government or, barring that, persuading the military to intervene once again.

Since none of the political tendencies would succeed in getting enough votes to win in the first round of the presidential contest, the election would be forced into a second round. At that point, the center would most likely ally with the left, further radicalizing the political process. It is apparent that under the first electoral option, Chile is more likely to structure a successful transition process. The second electoral option would not only lead to the election of a minority president, as the three political forces would go into the election divided, it would exacerbate political tensions and confrontations and would encourage the military to return to power under the banner of finishing the job they hoped to accomplish in 1973. With the second option, even if a president of the left is not elected, the likelihood of a military coup before 1997 must be placed at 55 percent. With a broader centrist option, by contrast, the likelihood of a coup would be around 20 percent and would depend on the civilian government's ability to contain extreme forces from both sides and accomplish critical policy objectives that would satisfy pent up social demands while maintaining a viable economy.[34]

Notes

1. See transitional Article 27 of the Constitution in Luz Bulnes Aldunate, *Constitución Política de la República de Chile: Concordancias, Anotaciones y Fuentes* (Santiago: Editorial Jurídica de Chile, 1981), p. 147.
2. See transitional Articles 17, 25, and 26, and article 95. With the election of the Senate, a year after the plebiscite is conducted, the Council of

State would cease to function, and the president of the Senate would
become a member of the National Security Council.

3. The elections would be held 30–45 days after being called. See
transitional Articles 28 and 29.

4. This section is based on interviews conducted in Santiago, in collabora-
tion with Pamela Constable, with close advisers to Pinochet who had a
hand in drafting the final version of the Constitution. Pinochet's
version met strong disapproval from Alessandri, who resigned his post
as council president in silence. Alessandri believed that a continuation
of military rule under Pinochet's direction would be detrimental to the
country and supported full implementation of the Constitution with its
provision for open elections by 1985. For a discussion of the drafting of
the Constitution and Alessandri's position, see Sergio Carrasco Delga-
do, *Génesis y Vigencia de los Textos Constitucionales Chilenos*, 2nd ed. (Santiago:
Editorial Jurídica de Chile, 1980).

5. For a reflection of this thinking, see the writings of Jaime Guzmán, the
brilliant Pinochet adviser and speech writer who was also a member of
the original commission set up to draft the Constitution. Particularly
revealing is his article "El Camino Político," *El Mercurio*, 26 December
1981, pp. C-4, 5.

6. The fairness of the 1980 referendum is the subject of considerable
controversy. Andrés Zaldívar, then-president of the centrist Christian
Democratic party, was exiled from Chile when he pointed to instances
of fraud. The absence of electoral registers, poll watchers, and an
independent electoral commission makes it impossible to confirm that
the electoral process was impartial.

7. As such, the chapter does not pretend to be a comprehensive overview
of recent Chilean political history. Background material can be found in
Pamela Constable and Arturo Valenzuela, "Is Chile Next?" *Foreign Policy*,
63 (Summer 1986), pp. 58–75, and Pamela Constable and Arturo
Valenzuela, "Plebiscite in Chile: End of the Pinochet Years?" *Current
History*, 87, no. 525 (January 1988), pp 29–33, 41. See also J. Samuel
Valenzuela and Arturo Valenzuela (eds.), *Military Rule in Chile: Dictatorship
and Oppositions* (Baltimore: Johns Hopkins University Press, 1986).

8. The observations in the text are based on interviews and conversations
with recently retired high-ranking military officers including the chiefs
of staff of the navy, army and national police, and lower-ranking
active-duty officers. It is difficult to overstate the importance that the
Chilean military attributes to the Constitution and the legal process. On
the political thought of the Chilean military, see Augusto Varas, Felipe
Aguero, and Fernando Bustamante, *Chile, Democracia, Fuerzas Armadas*
(Santiago: Facultad Latinoamericana de Ciencias Sociales, 1980). See
also Genaro Arriagada Herrera, "The Legal and Institutional Framework
of the Armed Forces in Chile," in J. Samuel Valenzuela and Arturo

Valenzuela (eds.), *Military Rule in Chile: Dictatorship and Oppositions* (Baltimore: Johns Hopkins University Press, 1986), and Arriagada Herrera's *La Política Militar de Pinochet* (Santiago: Salesianos, 1985).

9. These observations and others relating to perceptions by Chilean political leaders are based on extensive interviews conducted by the author in Santiago from 1982 to 1988.

10. The National Accord, signed by eleven political parties in August 1985, implicitly called for extensive constitutional changes, including competitive elections and a strong Congress. It was a powerful blow to Pinochet because its signatories included two parties whose members had backed the coup and strongly supported the government for many years, the National party and the National Union party.

11. Perhaps one of the most revealing documents is the humorous list of ten attributes for a good rightist submitted anonymously by an "outstanding leader of a rightist party" to a Chilean newsweekly. They included the following: "The good rightist believes Pinochet should go in '89, but he is not willing to kick him out"; "the good rightist would like to have a better option than Pinochet, but is unwilling to create one for fear that the 'chief might get mad'"; "the good rightist hopes to be shown that Pinochet is in fact the best option, and thus have an 'excuse' to vote for him." See "El Buen Derechista," *Qué Pasa*, 2–9 July 1987, p. 5. In interviews conducted by the author in Santiago, political leaders confirmed that some prominent citizens have been approached about their willingness to be an alternative candidate to Pinochet in the plebiscite. None was willing to take the step, for fear of losing and having to endure the potential repercussions.

12. Versions of the instructions to local officials were circulated widely in Santiago and were reproduced in several magazines.

13. A prominent U.S. academic with ties to the U.S. Republican party found on a trip to Santiago that his talk show interview was boycotted by the panelist from the right and that an interview in a prominent newspaper was censored.

14. Since Pinochet is both the commander in chief of the army and president of the republic, he would have two votes on the National Security Council; in the event of a tie, he would have a third vote because as president he could break a tie. Pinochet also appoints the comptroller general and the head of the Council of State, both of whom would be likely to vote for him. The current president of the Supreme Court would probably vote against Pinochet, though any of his likely successors would probably support the general and may very well be in place by the time the selection process occurs. Pinochet could thus obtain a majority in the council even if all of the other military commanders were against him. It is likely, then, that the other commanders will go along with Pinochet to avoid bringing the matter

before the National Security Council, which would threaten a division in the armed forces. However, they will attempt to extract a key concession from the president: that he step down as commander of the army if he receives the nomination. Pinochet might accept giving up the command on his inauguration for a new presidential term, but is very unlikely to do so in order to become the government nominee. This way he could keep his army command if he lost the election, and give it up if he won. It is instructive that the commanders have not repeated an earlier allusion to the fact that the candidate should be "in his fifties" (Pinochet is seventy-three), but continue to repeat that the candidate should be a civilian.

15. Pinochet would not be able to run for president himself should the designated candidate be defeated. The Constitution allows him a second term only if he is the candidate chosen to run in the plebiscite.

16. Article 96 describes the functions of the National Security Council. Transitional Article 8 establishes that the commanders of the armed forces and the director general of the national police will not be limited to a four-year term, as established in Article 93 of the Constitution. Rather, they will be limited to a four-year term beginning in 1993; thus, they will remain in office until 1997.

17. For General Leigh's account of his removal from the junta in what was nothing less than a coup within a coup, see Florencia Varas, *Gustavo Leigh: El General Disidente* (Santiago: Editorial Aconcagua, 1979). The involvement of Chilean security forces in international terrorism is described in John Dinges and Saul Landau, *Assassination on Embassy Row* (New York: Pantheon, 1980); and Taylor Branch and Eugene M. Propper, *Labyrinth* (New York: Viking, 1982).

18. Published reports that provide a glimpse of Pinochet's personality include Patricia Sethi's interview reproduced in the *LASA Forum*, 15, no. 2 (Summer, 1984).

19. It should be emphasized that the percentages reflect the probabilities of a Pinochet win or loss and not the projected results of the plebiscite. With a 40 percent chance of winning, Pinochet remains a formidable candidate.

20. Though the government has pledged that the opposition will have access to the media, the government campaign already in full swing is being conducted in an atmosphere of continued intimidation of the press. Numerous journalists have been indicted, one for publishing the remarks of a political leader who himself has not been charged with anything. The editor of the largest-circulation weekly magazine is serving a prison term for "defaming" the president. Opposition newspapers are finding that they cannot attract advertisers, for businessmen fear that if they place ads in those organs they might jeopardize their access to state credit and government subsidies.

Television is still firmly in the hands of pro-government organizations. Film clips showing riots and disorder from the past have been effectively used by pro-government propagandists.

21. Public opinion polls give strong support to this statement. In one survey, 70 percent of the population supported a return to democracy for Chile, while only 5.2 percent favored authoritarianism and 13.2 percent favored a continuation of the Pinochet regime. See Carlos Huneeus, *Los Chilenos y la Política* (Santiago: Centro de Estudios de la Realidad Contemporánea, 1986), p. 63. The best polling in Chile is now being carried out by Facultad Latinoamericana de Ciencias Sociales (FLACSO), with support from the National Endowment for Democracy. See FLACSO, *Informe de Encuesta: Opinión y Cultura Política* (Santiago: 1987). Other polling agencies include Geminis, Diagnos, and Testmerc. A poll conducted for the government by the Gallup organization has elicited considerable controversy. The results showed that 39.2 percent of respondents would vote yes, 26.6 percent would vote no, and 34 percent were undecided. The data suggested that the yes would lose in Santiago but win in the provinces. The problem with the poll is that although it was based on a national sample, the sample was not a representative one. For example, only 3.7 percent of the men in the sample were over 45 years old, whereas 41.3 percent of the women in the sample were over that age. The sample seriously overrepresents older citizens, particularly women. Poll results suggest that men and young people are more likely to vote no. The large undecided category in the poll is also problematic. See Gallup Chile, "Informe del Indice Gallup Chile" (Santiago: January 1988). The latest poll conducted in Santiago by the Centro de Estudios de la Realidad Contemporánea (CERC) indicates that the yes vote stands at 26.1 percent and the no vote at 44.1 percent, with the rest of the sample either undecided or unwilling to answer the question. See CERC "Informe Sobre Encuesta en Santiago" (Santiago: April 1988). An important trend in the latest poll is that support for the yes, which had been increasing in recent months, has leveled off. Also, more Chileans than before agreed that the no vote has a chance of winning. National polls conducted in April and June showed a much closer vote. While the no vote led by 30.2 percent in Santiago, the yes vote was ahead in cities having less that 150,000 inhabitants and was ahead 32.4 percent to 17.6 percent in cities with a population of less than 20,000. However, the number of respondents who refused to say who they would vote for still hovered over 30 percent, making the plebiscite difficult to call. The same polling group discovered that many Chileans admitted that they feared answering questions from pollsters, which may account for some of the undecided. See FLACSO, "Informe de Encuesta Nacional" (Santiago: 1988).

22. The results of the last competitive election, the congressional election of 1973, are reported in Arturo Valenzuela, *The Breakdown of Democratic Regimes: Chile* (Baltimore: Johns Hopkins University Press, 1978), p. 85.

23. For a brief discussion of these statistics, see Pamela Constable and Arturo Valenzuela, "Is Chile Next?" *Foreign Policy*, no. 63 (Summer 1986), pp. 58–75, and the comment of the Chilean ambassador in "Letters," *Foreign Policy*, no. 65 (Winter 1986–87), pp. 175–79.

24. Recent surveys suggest that the average Chilean does not consider some of the government's "economic modernization" measures, such as the privatization of the social security system, as beneficial as government economists believe they are. See Centro de Estudios Públicos, *Estudio Social y de Opinión Pública en la Población de Santiago* (Santiago: May 1987).

25. The party at first opposed all registration of its militants and supporters in the electoral rolls, arguing that any electoral contest would be a fraud and would play directly into the hands of the authorities and contribute to legitimizing the system. Soon, however, party leaders realized that long-time party activists could not accept a strategy that denied them the option of trying to defeat Pinochet peacefully at the polls. These observations are based on interviews with Communist party activists and attendance at public meetings in which party officials were admonished by their followers to change course.

26. So far the evidence is largely anecdotal. It stems from two sources: accounts from former government employees who were involved in fraudulent activities and opponents' observations of improper conduct, such as multiple voting by military units. There are also allegations that the figure for the final result was decided ahead of time and that government officials doctored the results from several regions. However, no systematic study of these allegations has been conducted.

27. One of the principal challenges for the opposition is to assure people that the vote will be secret and that the authorities will not be able to determine how they voted. Citizens still remember that in a plebiscite held in 1978, the ballots boxes were transparent and government polling officials could clearly see the voter's preference when the ballot was introduced into the ballot box. Even if opposition leaders are able to persuade voters that the actual ballot will be secret, given the small number of voters per polling place (350), local authorities could retaliate against individuals or neighborhoods whose polling places did not produce a winning margin for the government. Particularly in small and rural communities, where political allegiances and past voting patterns are easily identifiable, average citizens may not be fully confident that their vote will not be used against them.

28. The poll was conducted by Geminis in late August 1987. See Geminis, "Encuesta de Opiníon Pública" (Santiago: 1987).

29. In March 1987 a large portion of the Manuel Rodríguez Patriotic Front split from the Communist party after the party attempted to exercise greater control of what had been its loosely affiliated "military" wing. At the same time, the party came under strong pressure from followers to join the electoral process. A victory by the government candidate will only reinforce the insurrectionary tendencies on the left.

30. The authorities' contempt for the Congress is illustrated by the proposal to transfer it out of Santiago to the port city of Valparaíso and use the historic Congress building for other purposes.

31. Pinochet himself might lead a coup designed to close down Congress and restrict party activity while he retained his position as president. The general is a great admirer of former President José María Bordaberry of Uruguay, and would not hesitate to follow his example and try to rule directly with the armed forces, bypassing democratic procedures. It should be remembered, however, that Pinochet, if elected, would probably lose his position as commander in chief of the army. He would thus be more removed from the institution and more vulnerable to military action.

32. See the declaration of the fourteen parties that signed the agreement to support the no vote, "Declaración-Concertación de los Partidos Políticos por el No" (Santiago: February 2, 1988).

33. It was on the eleventh of September, 1973, that the Chilean armed forces overthrew the government of Socialist Salvador Allende. The date has an important symbolic meaning for regime supporters.

34. A center-right option during the transition process would not mean that the three sectors of Chilean politics would be rendered obsolete. Indeed, it is doubtful whether Chile will create a centrist and consensual politics in the near future. And it is likely that after the transition period is over, Chile's democratic politics would manifest some of the same deep divisions that led to the 1973 coup. However, it must be remembered that Chile also had one of the longest traditions of democratic governance in the world. If Chileans are able to structure a relatively consensual transition process, they should be able to return to the institutions that made the country distinctive and work on strengthening them for the future.

CHILE: THE LIMITS OF U.S. LEVERAGE

Susan Kaufman Purcell

Both the Carter and Reagan administrations have tried to get President Pinochet to leave power. Carter emphasized negative incentives or sanctions, hoping to punish and isolate Pinochet and thereby encourage him to step down. The policy did not work, although it made Americans feel good about themselves and helped win friends for the United States abroad. The Reagan administration, initially very critical of the Carter approach, tried to undo the "damage" by reversing Carter's policies and pursuing a more positive approach, or so-called quiet diplomacy. Pinochet did not change. When economic decline in Chile produced growing violence beginning in 1983, the U.S. adopted a more outspoken and active role in favor of a democratic transition in Chile, including largely symbolic sanctions in December 1987. The Reagan Administration is reluctant to impose harsher sanctions prior to the plebiscite. If Pinochet wins, however, pressure in the U.S. in favor of harsher sanctions will increase, despite the fact that such sanctions might do more harm than good.

The United States is faced with a familiar problem in Chile. General Augusto Pinochet Ugarte believes his continued rule is necessary to prevent a communist government from coming to power in his country. The Reagan administration believes that by prolonging his presidency, the general might bring about precisely the situation he claims to want to prevent. There are, after all, precedents. In Cuba, Fulgencio Batista was replaced by Fidel Castro. More recently, the Sandinistas succeeded Anastasio Somoza in Nicaragua.

The political climate in Chile today still seems far from the conditions that preceded the downfalls of Batista and Somoza. General Pinochet counts among his supporters significant numbers of the rural and urban poor. His constituents also include important members of the private sector, as well as key elements in the armed forces, especially the army. These groups and individuals back him in part because they have generally benefited from the policies he has implemented, particularly in the economic realm, where his devotion to free market principles has produced steady economic growth, with the exception of two or three bad years in the early 1980s.

Some of the Chilean president's support, however, results from the perceived absence of a viable or credible democratic alternative to his rule. Chile's political parties have so far failed to convince many Chileans that their return to power would not also bring back the intensely ideological and polarized political climate that led to the 1973 coup against President Salvador Allende. Given this uncertainty, many people prefer to stay with "the devil they know."

Yet the possible occurrence in Chile of the kind of political polarization that led to the installation of communist governments in Cuba and Nicaragua cannot be ruled out. Frustration with prolonged one-man rule caused the Chilean Communist party in 1980 for the first time to advocate the violent overthrow of Pinochet, a position it has not repudiated despite its June 1988 decision to participate in the upcoming plebiscite. This endorsement of violence as an acceptable course of action is significant because Chile's is the strongest Communist party in South America in terms of electoral support, accounting for an estimated 15 percent of the country's electorate. Traditionally strong in parts of the organized labor movement, it now has a base among university students and urban slum dwellers as well. The party's youth wing is also involved with the Manuel Rodríguez Patriotic Front, a Marxist guerrilla group with about 3,000 supporters that has engaged in an escalating campaign of urban sabotage. And in the countryside, large caches of arms

stored for future use and traced to Cuba were discovered in
1986.

In view of these developments and their potential for
producing increased polarization and violence that could lead
to a communist takeover in Chile, the United States would
like to ensure that General Pinochet does not stay in power
beyond the expiration of his presidential term in March 1989.
If the past is any guide to the present and future, however, the
United States may have few options for decisively influencing
events in Chile that do not also create new threats to U.S.
interests there.

U.S. Policy Under Carter

The first U.S. president to recognize the difficulty of getting
General Pinochet to relinquish power was Ronald Reagan's
predecessor, Jimmy Carter. The Carter administration relied
almost exclusively on the use of negative incentives, or
sanctions, to accomplish its goal. The idea was apparently to
punish and isolate Chile because of its violations of human
rights, thereby making continuation of one-man rule costly,
while at the same time holding out the promise of good
relations and other rewards if the regime's human rights
performance improved and democracy were restored. U.S.
representatives therefore repeatedly voted against loans for
Chile in the World Bank and the Inter-American Development Bank. In the United Nations Commission on Human
Rights, Washington supported the appointment of a special
rapporteur for Chile. And high-ranking U.S. government
officials conspicuously received leaders of the main opposition political parties.

The Carter administration took additional steps after the
Chilean Supreme Court refused to extradite three officials
allegedly involved in the Washington murder of Orlando
Letelier, Chile's ambassador to the United States during the
Allende administration, and his assistant, Ronni Moffit.
Washington reduced the U.S. mission in Chile to one-fourth
its size and recalled the military mission. The administration

did not invite Chile to the 1980 inter-American naval exercises known as UNITAS, and it terminated military sales still in the pipeline. (Congress had prohibited arms sales and military training of officers in 1976.) Finally, the United States forbade new Export-Import Bank lending, as well as new guarantees for Chile by the Overseas Private Investment Corporation (OPIC).

The Carter administration's actions produced more of an impact in the United States than in Chile. They allowed the U.S. government and the American people to feel good again about U.S. foreign policy in the aftermath of the Vietnam War. With Chile, the United States was opposing a dictator and finally placing itself on the "right side." It also was making its foreign policy congruent with its domestic policy by supporting human rights and democracy both at home and abroad.

The sanctions approach also helped the United States win friends internationally, especially among democratic governments and among groups opposing dictatorial rule. In Latin America, in particular, it gave impetus to the transition from authoritarian to democratic rule that began during the Carter years.

In Chile, while the policy won friends for the United States among the democratic opposition parties of the center and center-left, its impact was otherwise minimal. The economy did not crumble, in part because U.S., Western European and Japanese commercial banks continued to lend generously to the country. Instead, Chile began to experience an economic boom. Pinochet's strength among key groups such as the military and business increased as a result. The growing economy ultimately translated into enough popular support for Pinochet to win approval in 1980 of a new, undemocratic constitution. Its immediate effect was to grant the president at least nine more years in power.

Shortcomings of the Carter Policy

Carter administration officials were fairly confident in the ability of U.S. sanctions to weaken the Pinochet government. They had, after all, seen the strategy work before. According to their interpretation, U.S. policy had been mainly responsible for the overthrow of President Allende in 1973. In particular, they believed that U.S. efforts to deprive Chile of loans from international financial institutions had made an important contribution to the economic deterioration that led to Allende's downfall. They had been critical when this policy had been used against Salvador Allende, a democratically-elected president. They had no such qualms regarding Augusto Pinochet, who was not that kind of president.

However, the Carter administration drew the wrong conclusions from the Allende period. First, it overestimated the extent to which actions taken by the U.S. government had been responsible for Allende's overthrow. Second, and related to the first error, administration officials greatly underestimated the importance of Chilean domestic political forces in the unraveling of the Allende presidency.

Allende was deposed by the Chilean military, in an attempt to prevent the country from sliding further into economic and political chaos, and to protect itself as an institution. The disintegration of the country's economy was an important factor in generating the political unrest, but it had not been caused primarily by U.S. behavior in multilateral lending institutions. In fact, the economic assistance that Chile lost from those sources was more than compensated for by Western European and Latin American aid.

The main causes of Chile's economic problems were Allende's economic policies and announced plans for socializing the economy. They produced unprecedented rates of inflation, fear among key business groups, and a general lack of confidence in the nation's economic future. The results were a halt to new investment in the economy, disinvestment, and capital flight.

The political situation also was very disturbing, as evidence mounted that Allende was losing power to the radical left-wing parties in his governing coalition. Increasing violence, efforts to arm peasant militias and to change some of Chile's political institutions, and the stockpiling of arms finally caused the increasingly divided military to act. As had happened so many times in other Latin American countries, political and economic disintegration, combined with rather explicit threats to the military as an institution, produced a military takeover.

Chile under Pinochet, however, was not Chile under Allende. The Carter administration was applying the policy of economic sanctions to a right-wing, personalistic dictatorship, backed by the armed forces, at a time when many Chileans still believed that Pinochet had restored stability, order, and economic growth. While Chileans did not necessarily approve of the methods that the Pinochet regime had used—particularly the murder of real and imagined supporters of Salvador Allende in the immediate aftermath of the coup—there is little doubt that large numbers of them had supported the military takeover in 1973 and continued to back the Pinochet government in the late 1970s.

In further contrast to the situation under Allende, there was considerable support for Pinochet's economic policies within Chile and abroad. During the years when the Carter administration was opposing World Bank loans to Chile, for example, domestic and foreign direct investment there increased. And as noted, foreign commercial banks also lent heavily to Chile.

Nor were Pinochet's policies considered a direct threat to the military as an institution, as Allende's had been. In fact, the reverse was true. Under Pinochet, the military became a highly privileged group, as its access to wealth and positions of power increased dramatically.

Had the Carter administration been less ideological in its approach to Chile and more attuned to the political and economic dynamics of the country, it might have avoided drawing inappropriate conclusions from the Allende period and overestimating its own ability to influence Pinochet. The next U.S. administration did not make the same mistakes, but its ideological blinders led it to commit serious errors of another kind.

U.S. Policy Under Reagan

The Reagan administration initially was very critical of U.S. policy toward Chile during the Carter presidency. It opposed the use of punitive policies against nondemocratic regimes that were friendly to the United States, since these regimes shared many of the strategic interests and goals of the United States. Yet there were aspects of the behavior of such governments that the United States could not condone or accept, particularly in the area of human rights. The best way for Washington to make its views known and produce a change in the undesirable behavior, according to the Reagan administration, was through the use of positive incentives and behind-the-scenes, or so-called quiet, diplomacy.

The first order of business for the United States, however, was to undo what Reagan officials regarded as the serious damage done to relations between the two countries during the Carter presidency. The United States therefore reversed most of Carter's policies. It began voting in favor of loans to Chile in the World Bank and the Inter-American Development Bank. It restored Export-Import Bank credits and OPIC loan guarantees. And it explored with Congress the possibility of lifting the ban against military sales to Chile. This last effort was based on the argument that the U.S. ability to influence Pinochet and the Chilean military was seriously weakened by the absence of an arms sales and military training program. Too many congressmen, however, believed that the removal of military sanctions would signal U.S. acceptance or approval of the Pinochet regime and, particularly, of its continued abuse of human rights. The sanctions remained in place.

But the Reagan administration did what it could on the symbolic level to change the kinds of signals that the United States sent to Chile. It stopped singling out the Pinochet regime for its human rights abuses and instead balanced its criticism of abuses in Chile with criticism of such abuses in communist countries. The high-level contacts with opposition party officials that had occurred during the Carter years were replaced by regular contacts with military officers. And Washington named as ambassador to Chile a political appointee who proved to be less critical of Pinochet than the Reagan administration itself.

The reversal in U.S. policy did not, however, change the behavior of President Pinochet. The Reagan administration was therefore no more successful than its predecessor had been. Nevertheless, it is not clear that Washington initially was greatly troubled by the lack of results. The administration viewed right-wing authoritarian regimes, unlike communist ones, as threatening to U.S. interests only if they lasted too long, thereby allowing a replay of the situations that had produced the Cuban and Nicaraguan revolutions. When President Reagan took office, Chile—which had been under Pinochet for more than seven years—still seemed a relatively calm and stable place.

The growing economic crisis in Chile soon changed that perception. By 1983, the decrease in copper prices and the government's faulty economic policies, combined with a generalized world recession, had caused a severe economic decline in the country. A collapse of credit, widespread bankruptcies, and very high levels of unemployment produced massive demonstrations against the government. The situation became serious enough to force the Pinochet government to enter into discussions with the democratic opposition, which it had refused to do until then. Unfortunately, the Democratic Alliance, composed mainly of the Socialist and Christian Democratic parties, read the government's willingness to talk as a sign of weakness and used the opportunity to demand Pinochet's resignation. The dialogue ended. The worsening economic and social situation led the president to impose a state of siege in November 1984.

With the situation in Chile becoming ever more polarized, the Reagan administration began to rethink its policy. Quiet diplomacy had not softened the Pinochet dictatorship nor brought about a democratic opening. A policy of pure sanctions, tried by President Carter, also had failed. The obvious conclusion was to fashion a more fine-tuned policy based on a combination of the two approaches.

By this time, the Reagan administration also was rethinking its overall approach to "friendly dictators." Specifically, several developments were moving Washington into a more outspoken and active role against right-wing rulers and in favor of democratic development.

In Latin America in particular, Reagan's first term had coincided with a spectacular transition from authoritarian to democratic government. Although the Reagan administration claimed to have played an important role in bringing about the transition, the change actually resulted more from internal political, economic, and social developments in these countries than from U.S. policy. The administration had, however, played a constructive role, as had the Carter administration, by being openly supportive of the establishment of democratic rule. This stance gave increased legitimacy, as well as political space, to democratic opposition movements and sent an important signal to the undemocratic forces that opposed them.

U.S. support for democracy abroad was, in the mid-1980s, a low-cost, high-benefit policy. In the early 1960s, democratically elected rulers in Latin America had seemed irresponsible, demagogic, and too enamored of left-wing ideas; the new democratic leaders of the 1980s, by contrast, seemed more responsible, less anti-American, and centrist. By supporting them, the United States was able to be on the "right side" of developments in Latin America while strengthening governments that did not threaten its own interests. Furthermore, this policy translated into increased approval of U.S. foreign policy both at home and abroad.

Washington had also learned an important lesson from events in El Salvador in the early 1980s. Initially, the Reagan administration had supported, or at least tolerated, right-wing dictatorships because there seemed to be no acceptable alternative. In the case of El Salvador, the United States had originally allied itself with right-wing military and civilian leaders because the Marxist ideology of the left was unacceptable and the center had been progressively destroyed by the civil war. Eventually, the Reagan administration realized that such a policy would not generate sufficient political support, either in El Salvador or at home. It then began to play a more active role in creating a democratic centrist alternative, with good results.

Similarly, in the Philippines, the United States had initially believed that the choice was between Ferdinand Marcos and a communist dictatorship. Congressional opposition to fraudulent electoral practices, combined with the growth of a civilian movement pressing for fair elections, moved the administration to more actively support democracy. The fall of Marcos and the victory of Corazón Aquino strengthened those forces within the Reagan administration that favored a general policy of active U.S. support for democratic development.

One additional development encouraged the administration to adopt a more active and outspoken role in support of a democratic transition in Chile: the situation in Nicaragua. The professed goals of U.S. policy there had been changing over time. By the mid-1980s, the administration had come to believe that the democratization of the Sandinista regime was necessary if Nicaragua was not to constitute a security threat to its neighbors and, by extension, to the United States. The fact that the Reagan administration began to push hard for democracy in Nicaragua and not in Chile allowed critics of its Nicaragua policy to accuse it of hypocrisy. To give credibility to, and build support for, that policy, Washington decided to take a stronger stand in favor of a democratic transition in Chile.

When Chile's main opposition parties signed the National Accord for a Transition to Full Democracy in August 1985, it became easier for the United States to implement such a policy. The Accord reflected a new sense of realism and maturity on the part of the democratic opposition. Unlike the earlier Democratic Alliance, which had excluded the right-of-

center parties, the Accord brought together parties of the
right, center, and left. The fact that the Accord, in contrast to
the Alliance, did not adopt a confrontational approach toward
the Pinochet regime made possible its signing by the more
conservative parties. At the same time, because the Accord
proposed a number of constitutional reforms that implied an
end to Pinochet's indefinite rule, the more left-of-center
parties accepted it.

In addition, the Accord sought to assure the military and
other groups that a return to democracy would not bring back
the conflict and insecurity of the Allende years. It guaranteed
private ownership, expressed support for combating terrorism
and opposed collective trials of the military, such as those
occurring in neighboring Argentina. Furthermore, it called for
the immediate restoration of public liberties and the beginning of a process of transition to democracy.

Shortly after the signing of the Accord, the United States
named a new ambassador to Chile. Ambassador Harry Barnes
was a career foreign service officer rather than a political
appointee. In Chile, this difference was taken as a signal that
U.S. policy was changing. From the beginning, Ambassador
Barnes spoke strongly and publicly of the need for a return to
democracy in Chile. He established contacts with a broad
range of opposition politicians and simultaneously worked to
sustain his access to government officials. Then, in the spring
of 1986, the United States took the unprecedented step of
sponsoring a resolution in the United Nations Commission on
Human Rights denouncing human rights abuses in Chile. At
about the same time, President Reagan announced that "the
American people believe in human rights and oppose tyranny
in whatever form, whether of the left or the right." Soon after,
when Donald Regan was asked on a television program
whether the United States was trying to destabilize the
Chilean regime, he answered that no such effort was under
way "at [that] moment."

The spring of 1986 seemed to promise an ever more active
U.S. policy in support of a democratic transition in Chile. But
the discovery in August of that year of eight arms caches in

the countryside containing seventy tons of weapons, and the assassination attempt on Pinochet the next month, apparently caused second thoughts among some members of the Reagan administration. When Pinochet reimposed the state of siege, the United States tried to delay a vote on a World Bank structural adjustment loan for Chile. After its effort failed, the United States abstained from the November 1986 vote. It did not vote against the loan, although during the previous state of siege it had threatened to do so unless the state of siege were lifted. And as U.S. officials continued to make public declarations favoring a return to democracy in Chile, General Pinochet launched his "campaign" to succeed himself.

U.S. Policy and the Plebiscite

According to the 1980 Constitution, which remains in effect, a plebiscite on a presidential candidate must be held no later than February 1989. The candidate is to be selected unanimously by the four commanders in chief of the armed services (of whom Pinochet is one), 30–60 days before the vote. If the commanders cannot reach a unanimous decision, the choice will be made by the National Security Council, a somewhat broader group composed of both military and civilian officials. If the candidate selected by either process is not approved in the plebiscite, open, competitive elections will be held within a year.

Initially, democratic parties opposed to Pinochet's continuation in power condemned the plebiscite and demanded instead free and fair elections. Some joined with the nondemocratic opposition in mass demonstrations in support of such elections. At the same time, however, the democratic opposition parties urged their followers to register to vote in the scheduled plebiscite. This would enable them to vote against Pinochet if the government refused to allow free and fair elections. It would also enable opposition party members to serve as poll watchers in order to help prevent fraud.

This two-pronged strategy proved to be confusing and, ultimately, self-defeating, since it exacerbated conflicts within the democratic opposition and called attention to its disunity. In January 1988, in recognition of these problems, the Christian Democrats abandoned their campaign for democratic elections and instead urged their followers to vote no in the plebiscite. Their decision was also influenced by strong indications that Pinochet would not allow a free and open election for president. A month later, most of the center-left opposition parties joined the campaign for the no.

The focus of the campaign was the registration of new voters. It was based on the assumption that most unregistered voters were young and opposed to Pinochet. The organizers of the campaign believed that if they could register 6 million of the 8 million Chileans eligible to vote by September 1988, their chances of defeating Pinochet in a plebiscite would be good. By summer 1988, they had achieved their goal. Their success was impressive, given that the rules were skewed against them. In order to register, people had to spend considerable time and money. It had, of course, been the government's intent to thus discourage registration.

Polls taken this year, however, do not necessarily bear out the opposition's assumption that most newly registered voters will vote against Pinochet. Those who plan to vote no and those who say they will vote yes if Pinochet is the candidate are more or less evenly divided. The striking and unforeseen finding is the large percentage of voters—approximately one-third—who claim they are undecided. Given the undemocratic nature of Chile's political system, the large undecided segment may reflect fear or reluctance to express an intention to vote against the government. On the other hand, it may reflect true indecision. While many Chileans want an end to one-man rule, they do not necessarily have confidence that the opposition parties would give Chile either political stability or the economic policies that have brought the country uninterrupted growth for the past four years.

Their dilemma might have been avoided had the opposition united behind a right-of-center civilian candidate who was a committed democrat and who would have been acceptable to the military. This was the preferred option of three of the commanders of the armed services, announced when polls began showing that Pinochet would receive only about 20 percent of the vote in a plebiscite in which voters were asked to vote for or against him. The military understandably did not want to back a weak candidate whose loss in the plebiscite would plunge the country into uncertainty until new, competitive elections could be held one year later, as required by the Constitution. Pinochet's unflinching determination to be the candidate, however, combined with the inability of the opposition parties to unite around an alternative, ultimately caused the commanders to return to the fold and back Pinochet.

During this period, the United States stepped up its efforts to encourage a peaceful transition to democratic rule in Chile. In December 1987, the State Department, with the explicit approval of the White House, issued a strong statement calling for a lifting of Chile's state of exception and the establishment of broad democratic freedoms, including freedom of expression and assembly and equitable access to the media, especially television. Implicit in the statement was acceptance of a plebiscite in lieu of an open election. Also implicit, however, was a warning that the United States might reject the announced result of the plebiscite if it were produced by fraudulent or undemocratic behavior on the part of the regime.

At the same time, the Agency for International Development awarded a $1.2 million grant to the Center for Free Elections in Latin America, a nonpartisan organization based in Costa Rica that is dedicated to registering eligible voters for elections. The center, in turn, made a grant to Civitas, an independent foundation in Chile with strong links to the Catholic church. The grant partially reflected the assumption that the higher the number of registered voters, the greater the chances of defeating Pinochet. In addition, it reflected the belief that the results of the electoral process would be more legitimate if a large percentage of eligible voters participated in it.

The United States also made a special effort to help the democratic opposition offset its disadvantage of having to organize and operate in an undemocratic context in which the incumbent president enjoyed all the advantages. Specifically, in December 1987, Congress, with strong support from the executive, approved a $1 million special appropriation for the National Endowment for Democracy, much of which was to be used in Chile to support the activities of the democratic opposition. The funds, which began to reach Chile in May 1988, were to be used for advertising, polling, and other activities.

Complementing its emphasis on the democratic transition process, the United States continued to press for an improvement in Chile's human rights performance. In this area, Washington's leverage was particularly limited. Congress had forbidden military assistance and training since 1976, because of persistent human rights abuses by the Pinochet government. This left the Reagan administration with little to offer the Chilean military in the way of incentives. As a result, U.S. efforts to end human rights abuses in Chile involved mainly threats of sanctions and, eventually, their imposition in a mild form.

In the fall of 1987, for example, the United States once again abstained on a World Bank loan vote. However, Chile's human rights situation was better than it had been in 1986, when the United States had also abstained. Many exiles had returned, opposition newspapers were publishing, and opposition parties were registering voters and campaigning. The abstention, therefore, represented a toughening of the U.S. position, while still falling short of actually imposing sanctions.

Shortly after the World Bank vote, the Reagan administration for the first time did impose limited economic sanctions on Chile. In order for a country to participate in the General System of Preferences (GSP) and OPIC programs, it must meet international standards of behavior in the area of labor rights. In December 1986, the United States had put Chile on probation for failing to meet these standards. By December

1987, Chile had not made the changes it had promised to make, so the United States removed GSP benefits from approximately $40 million of Chilean exports and suspended Chile's eligibility for OPIC guarantees.

On the one hand, the sanctions are largely symbolic. According to a 1987 study by the Congressional Research Service of the Library of Congress, commissioned by Congressman Douglas Bereuter, the proportion of Chilean goods entering the United States with the GSP duty-free status was 4.48 percent in 1985 and 6.35 percent in 1986. The prohibition of OPIC loan guarantees also will be tolerable, since Chile received none of these between 1984 and 1987. On the other hand, the sanctions do send a warning signal to both the Pinochet government and the private sector, which has remained essentially loyal to Pinochet and has not actively supported a return to democracy.

The Reagan administration is reluctant to adopt additional sanctions against Chile before the plebiscite for several reasons. The United States does not want to damage the Chilean economy, especially since the Pinochet government has been implementing the kind of free market policies advocated by the Baker plan, and with good results. In 1987, for example, the economy grew by more than 5 percent, with the same rate projected for 1988. Inflation was 21 percent in 1987 and is expected to decrease to 8–10 percent this year. In addition, Chile has been a leader in the conversion of portions of its multi-billion-dollar debt into equity and is attracting substantial foreign investment. Compared with most of its neighbors, therefore, Chile is a great economic success story.

Furthermore, U.S. adoption of more severe economic sanctions against Chile could provide Pinochet with a perfect excuse for recentralizing the economy, increasing the economic role of the state, and repudiating the national debt. This last move in particular would substantially increase his popular support, as well as allow him to end Chile's isolation from the democratic governments of Latin America. Pinochet, after all, chose to implement free market policies not because he is a confirmed capitalist, but because doing so enabled him to revive Chile's economy and thereby facilitate his own consolidation of political power. If the United States were to impose harsh sanctions, Pinochet would do what he deemed necessary to save himself and his regime.

Finally, harsh economic sanctions constitute the only remaining tool with which the United States can press for both improvements in human rights and a transition to democracy in Chile. It makes little sense to try and impose such sanctions while Chile is in the midst of an electoral process that could produce a peaceful transition toward democracy. It is at least conceivable—although, admittedly, not highly probable—that Pinochet could accept defeat in the plebiscite and allow free and competitive elections for president the following year.

If Pinochet wins the plebiscite, however, the argument for imposing sanctions will become more compelling, at least for those in the United States who will be convinced that his victory is the result of fraud. (It may or may not be the case that fraud is the only way for Pinochet to win; he does, in fact, enjoy significant support, particularly in rural areas and in small towns.) Even so, it is far from clear that sanctions will solve the political problem even though they could have severe economic effects.

In the past, when Chile's main export was copper, which was both fungible and nonperishable, and the country was less dependent on outside capital and investment, the country was less vulnerable. Today, in contrast, Chile exports large amounts of fruits, vegetables, and other perishable products to the United States—products that often have been tailored to the tastes of the American consumer. And the liberal economic reforms implemented during Pinochet's rule have made the Chilean economy much more open and, consequently, much more vulnerable to outside efforts to destabilize it.

It is precisely because sanctions could indeed now cause severe damage to the Chilean economy that their wisdom and desirability must be questioned. The recent unfortunate experience with U.S. sanctions against Panama provides a good example of the limitations of such a policy. If the imposition of sanctions were to play out in the same way in Chile, the result would be a wrecked economy, an increase in anti-Americanism, and Pinochet's continuation in power.

The decision of what to do about Chile in the event of a fraudulent Pinochet victory will not, in any event, be made by the Reagan administration. The next U.S. administration will decide what course of action to pursue. And the decision will be in the hands not only of the new president, but also of a Congress controlled by a Democratic party that, if Panama and South Africa are examples, continues to believe that the possible benefits to the United States of economic sanctions outweigh the risks. Both the next U.S. president and Congress should bear in mind, however, that the ability of the United States to play a constructive role in any democratic transition process in Chile ultimately will depend on the behavior of the Chilean people. The United States can only follow their lead; it cannot, and should not, get out in front of them.

CHRONOLOGY OF EVENTS

1958   Independent-Conservative Jorge Alessandri wins the presidency in a field of five candidates with 31.2 percent of the vote. He defeats Socialist Salvador Allende, the runner-up, by only 33,000 votes, less than 3 percent of the votes cast.

1964   Christian Democrat Eduardo Frei is elected president with the support of rightist parties in a two-way race. Allende polls 38.6 percent of the vote to Frei's 55.7 percent. Frei, with strong economic and political support from the United States, presides over a "revolution in liberty," instituting wide-ranging reforms.

1970   Salvador Allende is elected president with 36.2 percent of the vote, defeating Alessandri (34.9 percent) and Christian Democrat Radomiro Tomic (27.8 percent). The Central Intelligence Agency tries to prevent Allende from assuming the presidency. General René Schneider, Commander in Chief of the Chilean Army, is killed in a kidnap attempt.

1971   Allende's Popular Unity coalition garners 48.6 percent of the vote in municipal elections, strengthening the determination of coalition parties to press for far-reaching socio-economic transformation.

1973   April: The Popular Unity coalition obtains the same percentage of the vote it had garnered in the previous congressional race, despite an atmosphere of growing confrontation and economic crisis.

        September 11: The Chilean armed forces depose President Salvador Allende, disband the Congress and all of the country's local governments. Army Commander Augusto Pinochet Ugarte becomes junta head.

1974   General Pinochet becomes Supreme Chief of the Nation, establishing his executive authority as distinct from that of the legislative junta, by virtue of Decree Law 527. With Decree Law 806, he takes the official title of President of the Republic.

1976   June 30: President Ford signs the Defense Appropriations Bill (1976–77), which contains a provision (the Kennedy-Humphrey Amendment) prohibiting the sale or grant of arms to Chile or the training of Chilean officers by U.S. officers.

        September 21: Orlando Letelier, Former Chilean Ambassador to the United States and his American assistant, Ronni Moffitt, are killed by a car-bomb in Washington, D.C.

75

1977   Newly-elected U.S. President Jimmy Carter focuses his administra-
         tion's foreign policy on human rights and increasingly criticizes the
         abuses of the Pinochet government.

1979   February 14: Michael Townley, a U.S. citizen employed by the
         Chilean secret police (DINA), together with three Cuban exiles, is
         convicted in a U.S. federal court of the murders of Orlando Letelier
         and Ronni Moffitt. A United States request for the extradition of
         DINA head General Manuel Contreras is denied by the Chilean
         Supreme Court.

1980   September 11: A new constitution is approved by 67 percent of the
         electorate. However, the plebiscite is marred by the lack of voter
         registration rolls and mechanisms for assuring the reliability of the
         final count. The Constitution gives Pinochet another eight-year
         term and sets up a series of institutions and provisions aimed at
         restricting democratic practices.

1981   The Reagan adminstration decides to take a less confrontational
         stance toward the Pinochet government, increasing its ties with the
         Chilean military and toning down the criticism of the past four
         years.

1983   Following a year when the economic growth rate fell by 14.2
         percent, massive protests break out, forcing the regime to make
         concessions of greater openness and participation.

1985   August 11: Under the sponsorship of the Archbishop of Santiago,
         Juan Francisco Fresno, 11 political parties ranging from right to left
         sign a National Accord for a Transition to a Full Democracy. The
         Accord calls for free and open elections, rather than the yes or no
         plebiscite contemplated in the 1980 Constitution. The Accord breaks
         down, due to sharp divisions among the signatories.

1986   The United States abstains on a World Bank loan, due to the human
         rights situation in Chile and the lack of progress in returning to
         democratic government.

         September 7: An insurrectionary group linked to the Chilean
         Communist party nearly succeeds in assassinating President Pino-
         chet.

1987   Opposition political parties, with the exception of the Communist
         party, agree to register voters in the government registration rolls
         while pressing for free and competitive elections.

1988   Early in the year, opposition groups, with the exception of the
         Communist party, launch a campaign for the no vote in the
         plebiscite. In June the Communists decide to join the campaign.
         Polls reveal a close vote, with a large number of undecided voters.

Suggestions for Further Reading

In the first two or three years after the coup, more books and articles were published on Chile than in the previous 50. Since then, however, the number of titles has tapered off, and much of what is readily available in bookstores and libraries is outdated. Nonetheless, some valuable studies continue to appear in English, although the best recent work is still in Spanish.

Essential to an understanding of the Chilean setting and the immediate background to the military regime are Paul E. Sigmund, *The Overthrow of Allende and the Politics of Chile, 1964-76* (Pittsburgh: University of Pittsburgh Press, 1977) and Arturo Valenzuela, *The Breakdown of Democratic Regimes: Chile* (Baltimore and London: The Johns Hopkins University Press, 1978). In addition to condensing a vast amount of material into less than 150 pages, the Valenzuela volume has the additional virtue of providing the most balanced assessment yet available on the Allende years.

Two collective volumes assess the Pinochet years from different perspectives; J. Samuel Valenzuela and Arturo Valenzuela, eds., *Military Rule in Chile: Dictatorship and Oppositions* (Baltimore and London: The Johns Hopkins University Press, 1986), and Gary M. Walton, ed., *The National Economic Policies of Chile* (Greenwich, Conn.: Jai Press, 1985). The brothers Valenzuela have brought together Chilean economists, political scientists and historians to evaluate the legacy of the military regime. Their findings are generally negative, particularly with regard to economic and social policy. Walton, who is dean of the business school at the University of California, Davis, has assembled a team of free market economists—again, mostly Chileans—who are generally supportive of the policies followed since 1973, but he also allows critics of those policies to have their say.

Both perspectives should be evaluated in the light of the recent report of the World Bank, *Social Indicators of Development, 1987* (Washington, D.C.: The World Bank, [September,] 1987).

Three books explore the relationship between the regime and various sectors of Chilean society: Brian Smith, *The Church and Politics in Chile: Challenges to Modern Catholicism* (Princeton, N.J.: Princeton University Press, 1982); Genaro Arriagada, *La Política Militar de Pinochet* (Santiago de Chile: Salesianos, 1986); and Carlos Huneeus, *Los Chilenos y la Política: Cambio y Continuidad en el Autoritarismo* (Santiago de Chile: Centro de Estudios de la Realidad Contemporánea, 1986). Smith provides a longer view of church-state relations and Catholic social thought in relation to economic and social policies going back to the 1920s. Arriagada, one of Chile's most distinguished political scientists, examines promotion patterns and other changes in the structure and doctrine of the Chilean army since 1973. Carlos Huneeus looks at currents of political opinion over time, and finds that Chileans of all social classes have changed remarkably little in their basic convictions since the 1950s.

Chile Study Group

June–December, 1987

Stephen W. Bosworth, Group Chairman
Mark Falcoff, Group Director
Susan Kaufman Purcell, Director, Latin American Project
Theodore Piccone, Rapporteur
Stephanie R. Golob, Rapporteur for Fifth Meeting

First Meeting: June 9, 1987

Discussion Leaders
Edgardo Boeninger, Centro de Estudios del Desarrollo, Chile
Sergio Bitar, Centro Latinoamericano de Economía y Política Internacional,
    Chile
Mark Falcoff, Council on Foreign Relations

Second Meeting: September 9, 1987

Discussion Leaders:
Harry G. Barnes, Jr., U.S. Ambassador to Chile
José Miguel Barros, former Chilean Ambassador to the Netherlands, the
    United States and Peru
Susan Kaufman Purcell, Council on Foreign Relations

Third Meeting: October 21, 1987

Discussion Leaders:
George W. Landau, former U.S. Ambassador to Chile (1977–1982)
Nathaniel Davis, former U.S. Ambassador to Chile (1971–1973)
Fernando Leniz, former Minister of Finance of Chile

Fourth Meeting: November 19, 1987

Discussion Leaders
Erich Schnacke, Chilean Socialist Party (Núñez)
Andrés Zaldívar, Chilean Christian Democratic Party

Fifth Meeting: December 10, 1987

Discussion Leaders:
Lucía Santa Cruz de Ossa, Historian and Member, Editorial Board, *El
    Mercurio*
Arturo Valenzuela, Georgetown University

Group Members

Harry G. Barnes, Jr., U.S. Ambassador to Chile
Peter Bell, Edna McConnell Clark Foundation
Richard Bloomfield, World Peace Foundation
Lt. Col. Henry Bream, USAF, Office of the Joint Chiefs of Staff
Raymond Brittenham, Lazard Frères & Co.
Henry Catto, Washington Communications Group
James Chace, Carnegie Endowment for International Peace
Greg Craig, Office of Senator Edward Kennedy
Curtis Cutter, Interworld Consultants, Inc.
William Doherty, American Institute for Free Labor Development
John C. Duncan, Cyprus Minerals Company
Richard Feinberg, Overseas Development Council
Devon Gaffney, Smith Richardson Foundation
Robert Gelbard, U.S. Department of State
Carl Gershman, National Endowment for Democracy
Robert Helander, Jones, Day, Reavis & Pogue
Lt. Col. David J. Hunt, USAF, Office of the Joint Chiefs of Staff
Stephen Kass, Berle, Kass & Case
Michael Kramer, *U.S. News & World Report*
Clifford Krauss, Edward R. Murrow Fellow, Council on Foreign Relations
Stanley Kwiesiak, Military Fellow, Council on Foreign Relations
George W. Landau, Americas Society
José Luis Llovio-Menéndez, Shepardson Fellow, Council on
  Foreign Relations
Ed Long, Office of Senator Tom Harkin
Frank McNeill, Consultant
Bruce Morrison, U.S. Congress (D., Conn.)
Martha T. Muse, The Tinker Foundation
Frederic C. Rich, Sullivan & Cromwell
Linda Robinson, *Foreign Affairs*
M.J. Rossant, The Twentieth Century Fund
Hewson Ryan, Fletcher School of Law and Diplomacy
Susan Segal, Manufacturers Hanover Trust
Sally Shelton-Colby, Bankers Trust Company
Paul E. Sigmund, Princeton University
Donald Strauss, Past President, American Arbitration Association
Peter Tarnoff, Council on Foreign Relations
Viron P. Vaky, Carnegie Endowment for International Peace
Jiri Valenta, University of Miami
Arturo Valenzuela, Georgetown University

About the Authors

Mark Falcoff is Resident Scholar in Foreign Policy at the American Enterprise Institute in Washington. He was a professional staff member with responsibility for Latin America on the Senate Foreign Relations Committee in the 99th Congress, and has taught at the universities of Illinois, Oregon and California (Los Angeles). His most recent book, *Modern Chile: A Critical History,* will be published this year.

Arturo Valenzuela is Professor of Government and Director of the Latin American Studies Program at Georgetown University. He is the author of numerous books and articles on Chilean politics, including *The Breakdown of Democratic Regimes: Chile.* Prior to joining the Georgetown faculty, he was Professor of Political Science at Duke Univeristy, and has been a visiting fellow at Oxford University, the University of Chile and the University of Sussex.

Susan Kaufman Purcell is Senior Fellow and Director of the Latin American Project at the Council on Foreign Relations in New York. She was a member of the Policy Planning Staff, U.S. Department of State, with responsibility for Latin America and the Caribbean (1980–1981). Prior to that, she was a professor of political science at the University of California, Los Angeles (1969–1979) and a visiting professor at Columbia University (1981).